It's the Thermostat, Stupid!

Every home and business has a thermostat,
yet no one really knows what it's doing
....at least until now!

Joel Gilbert, P.E.

It's the Thermostat, Stupid!

Every home and business has a thermostat, yet no one really knows what it's doing ....at least until now!

Am I implying you or the electric utility industry is stupid? Not at all! It's just a variation of the phrase, "It's the economy, stupid" coined by James Carville as campaign strategist for Bill Clinton's successful 1992 presidential campaign.

The phrase has become a cliché in American political culture to establish what the speaker believes the real problem to be. Examples include "It's the deficit, stupid," "It's the corporation, stupid," "It's the math, stupid," and "It's the voters, stupid!"

So, please, don't be offended. I chose the title to pointedly grab your attention and shift focus. As in the campaign that made the phrase famous, this captures the "ah ha!" moment, the blinding flash of the obvious I think you'll feel when you read this book. You will say, "Wow! Why didn't I see this before?"

It's not been obvious to any of us involved in the utility industry because our viewpoint has been trapped in the meter-centered paradigms of the utility business.

The Traditional Meter Data Paradigm

Meters are obviously important to the electric utility industry. They are the cash register of the business and are the primary data source for creating the monthly bill customers receive. Residential electric meters only register energy consumption in kWh. The recent emphasis on graphing this data and presenting it to customers seems unarguable. After all, anything has to be better than just getting a bill once a month.

Seeing the actual energy use each hour appeals to those who understand how energy is used in a typical home. But, it is a great big yawn to most customers since there are so many things that use electricity in a home. It is almost impossible to determine what is operating each hour of the day. Plus, who cares … really. Customers want to know what they can do about it.

Now, after several years of utilities in the US and abroad attempting to make this useful and interesting to consumers, it is about time to question traditional meter data as a customer engagement premise.

Imagine checking out at the grocery store and seeing the total bill is $150, but you have no idea what you put in the basket or how much each item costs. Worse yet, you are not aware of why some of those items in your cart cost as much as they do or what you can do about that cost in the future.

The past few years have also witnessed the attempt to answer these types of metering questions with smaller and smaller electric meter intervals and enhanced meter accuracies. The thought was that by going to 15-minute, 5-minute, or even 1-minute recording intervals, the electric use patterns would come to life and engage customers. While these enhanced resolutions do help the technical type customers see things like refrigerators cycling during the quiet times of the night and can certainly spot things like electric heating systems turning on and off, they are often clouded by the fog of all the other appliances operating in the home.

The truth is, customers do not care about seeing the refrigerator cycling at night. They are not going to change behavior by seeing that data. That information simply clouds the other data making real behavior changing decisions impossible.

Shift to a Thermostat Monitoring Paradigm

This book presents an alternative approach that unlocks enormous engagement potential. In most homes, it's the thermostat on the heating and cooling system that controls the largest energy uses. Monitoring and reporting information about those thermostats (temperature and time data) is shown as a powerful consumer education channel. It is much better than the meter. And, it puts the customers in charge of their consumption. They learn what they can do to affect change in their usage and the cost, and they see results right away.

Still, the meter plays an important role. It is the scoreboard in the energy game. It measures how much electricity the home uses. But watching it is not any more engaging than watching the scoreboard in a competitive match. The action is on the playing field, and the engagement we are looking for will come from the thermostat information, not the meter. Perhaps with this paradigm shift, we might break through the other customer engagement challenges that have plagued the energy industry for decades.

We've been showing customers the score and trying to make it interesting, hoping the scoreboard will engage them. It hasn't…and how many millions of dollars and hours have been spent trying? It's time for a shift to a thermostat-centric view, telling homeowners how they are playing the energy game by showing them how their thermostats operate in their homes.

Another Example of Acres of Diamonds

The story reprinted here from Nightingale Conant is true: It is told of an African farmer who heard tales about other farmers who had made millions by discovering diamond mines. These tales so excited the farmer that he could hardly wait to sell his farm and go prospecting for diamonds himself. He sold the farm and spent the rest of his life wandering the African continent searching unsuccessfully for the gleaming gems that brought such high prices on the markets of the world. Finally, worn out and in a fit of despondency, he threw himself into a river and drowned.

Meanwhile, the man who had bought his farm happened to be crossing the small stream on the property one day, when suddenly there was a bright flash of blue and red light from the stream bottom. He bent down and picked up a stone. It was a good-sized stone, and admiring it, he brought it home and put it on his fireplace mantel as an interesting curiosity.

Several weeks later a visitor picked up the stone, looked closely at it, hefted it in his hand, and nearly fainted. He asked the farmer if he knew what he'd found. When the farmer said, no, that he thought it was a piece of crystal, the visitor told him he had found one of the largest diamonds ever discovered. The farmer had trouble believing that. He told the man that his creek was full of such stones, not all as large as the one on the mantel, but sprinkled generously throughout the creek bottom.

The farm the first farmer had sold, so that he might find a diamond mine, turned out to be one of the most productive diamond mines on the entire African continent. The first farmer had owned, free and clear ... acres of diamonds. But he had sold them for practically nothing, in order to look for them elsewhere. The moral is clear: If the first farmer had only taken the time to study and prepare himself to learn what diamonds looked like in their rough state, and to thoroughly explore the property he had before looking elsewhere, all of his wildest dreams would have come true.

This story that has so profoundly affected millions of people is relevant because each of us is, at this very moment, standing in the middle of our own acres of diamonds. If we only had the wisdom and patience to intelligently and effectively explore the work in which we're now engaged and to explore ourselves, we would most likely find the riches we seek, whether they be financial or intangible or both.

Before you go running off to what you think are greener pastures, make sure that your own is not just as green or perhaps even greener. It has been said that if the other guy's pasture appears to be greener than ours, it's quite possible that it's getting better care. Besides, while you're looking at other pastures, other people are looking at yours.

Getting Back on Message

How ironic that our diamonds in the rough have been buried in plain sight just as the ones in this African farmer's story. Everyone has been walking right by them. It's the intention of this book to point them out and let you better understand their beauty. Yes, the primary reason they can be mined today is that the cost of computing and communicating has dropped remarkably over the past few years. But, perhaps this "blinding flash of the obvious" is just one more example of how we humans can miss things that are right under our nose and in plain sight because we are focused on finding the answer in a certain place.

I liken it to how TV has improved over the past decades. I remember when it was first introduced in the mid-1950s. It was a small screen with fuzzy black and white images. You had to hold the antenna at a certain angle to get a good picture and it would fade in and out of clarity. Along came color TV! An improvement, but the colors were blurred. Then, in the late 60s, TVs got pretty good. The color was so impressive at the time, you would sit there glued to the set and watch almost anything. Now, with the advent of high definition TV, you can see the individual blades of grass and announcers on the news can't hide so easily behind makeup. If you look at a normal broadcast on a high definition TV, it looks horribly grainy. And, best of all, these high resolution TVs are getting so inexpensive that people are scattering them throughout their homes.

The same evolution has happened in temperature and humidity measurement. You could say, as a turn on an old energy industry phrase, it is now "too cheap *not* to meter^{SM}" the existing thermostat. And, by doing that you can detect and quantify almost everything a homeowner might care about that affects their comfort, their home energy performance, and of course, their energy bills.

What happens when you do take a closer look at the thermostat? First, you find yourself going back to the traditional utility paradigm to explain the electricity use. You will say, "Oh, sure, I get it ... the time the thermostat is on is proportional to the energy the HVAC system uses. Cool ... neat ... so all I have to do is to keep track of thermostat operating hours each day! Yea! Thanks!" Not so fast. That is another trap and misses the underlying details that are vital.

Think of this as the "Heartbeat of the Home[SM]." There is a rich rhythm of information in this detail. And, it is now so inexpensive to monitor, you can't afford not to. Prices will continue to drop, of course, but even now we are at price points under $30 to accurately monitor a thermostat. Best news of all is that this device can be applied to any existing thermostat, and there is "Nothing to Install … Just Stick it to the Wall[SM]!"

I believe customers will become increasingly interested in this information. Thermostat monitoring enables us to "Dollarize the Degrees[SM]," or show in dollars how much that extra degree or two cost each day. They will see how much holding 72 degrees costs on a summer day vs. setting the control point up to 78 or 80 degrees. Translating each degree to a dollar amount each day can make a difference in customer behavior.

Then, as residents do become engaged, they can go the next step and wire it into their existing thermostat, convert that to a communicating programmable thermostat, and start managing the largest energy user in most homes by truly becoming engaged in its operation. Now, at last, we can truly engage homeowners with energy information.

That is what this book is about. Please accept my invitation to explore these new dimensions of a Thermostat Centered Paradigm (**TCP**). As you will see, it complements the traditional **Meter Centered Paradigms** (**MCP**). MCPs are great scoreboards but they simply do not tell you how you are playing the energy game. We've spent way too much time and resources trying to convince customers to watch the scoreboard. Let's get going now on getting them engaged with energy in a way that is empowering and relevant to customers.

This approach also produces some interesting new value propositions for our industry.

> **Energy Efficiency Advocates:** We can now isolate and communicate how each HVAC system in the home and even the water heater are behaving. We can document and define improvements programs make on energy structures (the asset) and truly separate those from behavior (thermostat settings). We can inform and empower customers to engage in an ongoing dialogue since they do understand temperature and time. And, perhaps most importantly, we can troubleshoot "failures" to save money when houses are improved.

> For example, how can this happen: The homeowner weatherized the home, but the bills remain high. Why did the investment in insulation, air sealing and a new heating or cooling system produce no savings? This device will pinpoint if occupants took back the savings in improved comfort by changing thermostat settings and to what extent the home's

physical structure and HVAC equipment was improved.

Demand Response Advocates: Reducing energy use during those hot summer afternoons is often an electric energy company or an electricity retailer priority. Traditionally, it has been expensive to engage customers in these programs because it was essential to know how much the customer's energy use declined during those periods of time. Finally, we can know for sure what a house can do and when they actually can and did do it. We can engage customers with an old thermostat in programs and let them know precisely what they did … even those with window air conditioners that don't seem to have a thermostat. And, we don't need interval meters … we can do this with traditional meters read once a month!

This is just the beginning of a fascinating period of renewal and discovery in an industry that, frankly, has gotten pretty intellectually stale. Fortunately, the energy industry is brimming with intelligent people. It's my hope this book will set the stage for a completely new focus and a renewed look at energy engagement.

Table of Contents

Chapter 1   1
Getting over the Electric Meter Paradigm

Chapter 2   23
Thermostat Monitoring – The Heartbeat of the Home^{SM}

Chapter 3   51
The Changing Utility Customer Relationship

Chapter 4   65
Demand Response – A New Resource Pool?

Chapter 5   81
Residential and Small Commercial DR Liquidity

Chapter 6   101
"Things may come to those who wait …"

Chapter 1:

Getting over the Electric Meter Paradigm

I f you work in or around the electric utility industry, you know the industry is centered around meters. The industry has even labeled customers as meters with phrases like: "We serve 100,000 meters." This is changing of course. But, even today, the energy utility industry only talks about kW, kWh, or Btus per month when describing customer energy use.

The hope with advanced communicating electric meters (a.k.a. the Smart Grid) and the recent $6 billion in ARRA government funding for the smart grid coupled to the US Government's promotion of the Green Button was that it would engage Americans better than once-a-month bill information. Once you set aside the 1-2% that are interested in anything and everything about energy use in the home, the engagement statistics are dreadful. It has not proven to be any more informative, engaging or motivational to the masses.

I think I can explain why if you will lower your emotional resistance to change and stop being so defensive about the value of these new meters and information platforms. I get it. I too started as a Smart Grid advocate for all the obvious reasons. It has to be better than once-a-month aggregate bills. The opportunities for alerts and alarms clearly are superior to waiting until the end of the month for a billing update. Time based energy use incentives are clearly better than flat pricing models, especially when the few hours of summer and/or winter peak conditions could be improved by customer actions for just a few hours. Plus, there are so many sound business improvements possible through the smarter grid that surrounds the smart meters. It just makes good business sense ... and it may ... but the engagement of the customer has always been an afterthought.

My wife, Susan, and I attended a utility industry conference on the Smart Grid and were excited to see there was a discussion session on the customer experience one afternoon. Only one other person showed up out of the 150 in attendance! The tables covering meter data management, meter to cash, cyber security and other topics were jammed. The subject of the customer experience was just not that interesting to the industry.

The business reasons are, of course, centered on the business processes: reading the meter and producing bills. Yes, there are added costs to the added information and some special challenges around the communications and database size, not to mention the rightful concerns over security as the historical electro-mechanical "dumb" meter is replaced with one that communicates electronically to the outside world. The business case is complex with lots of plus and minus elements, but virtually none of them are customer engagement.

The regulatory view of all this is quite different. Utility regulators have long hoped for advanced meters to offer customers better price signals than once a month aggregate billing parameters. After all, any economist worth his or her salt knows that it is inefficient to shield customers from price, especially when it varies as much as it does in the electric utility industry. Prices can be near-zero at night and well past $1.00 per kWh during brief heat storms ... how can anyone feel good about averaging those extremes into some form of an average price for all kWh consumed?

Better meter data surely solves the problem! Hourly data? Quarter Hour? Every Minute?

Some of you are no doubt clinging to another hope. Surely finer detail in the electric meter data can bring all this to life and engage consumers. There are several companies offering room by room energy monitoring and one major trade publication to the energy industry even commented that customers could notice the power use of the refrigerator light when it came on after opening the refrigerator door. Well, isn't that silly. Every time this customer entertained themselves by doing that they dumped more energy on the floor that they didn't know about with the meter ... the cold air in the refrigerator.

You must remember your parents or grandparents yelling at you when you peered into the refrigerator and took more than a few seconds keeping the door open. It seems like only yesterday that my father yelled at me for keeping the front door to the house open for more than the absolute minimum to pass through it. The meter will not inform you about the real energy cost of keeping the door open. The light in the refrigerator is normally off. I think you are getting my point.

Once the utility business case for advanced metering clears the sniff test, the next rightful question is the level of detail that makes sense. Since electric utility prices change hourly in regional electricity markets, this seems to be the obvious choice from a billing point of view. That still means over 700 data points of information are compared to the traditional one summary reading each month. Oh my … 700 compared to 1. The industry also knows from its past with larger electricity customers that it would be better to have 15 minute intervals to let the customer know more about how they were using energy since hourly data resolution is a bit rough to interpret. 2800 compared to the historical 1.

And, while we are at it, why not consider 5 minute or even 1 minute intervals? Could it be that customer engagement is unleashed once the "picture is clear" to consumers how they use electricity? This makes some intuitive sense given the trends over time in the quality of TV we all watch. I remember when we were happy watching a grainy and fuzzy black and white TV and we had to keep moving the rabbit ear antenna to adjust the picture for each channel. We also had to get up out of our chair to change the channel, adjust the volume, etc. And, yes, I walked to school in knee deep snow uphill both ways.

But, seriously, do think about today's HD channels and how much you can now see. It is almost scary how much detail you can see in a person's face … every hair and every facial pore. Golf matches show every blade of grass and the tattoos on professional athletes are completely discernible. If we got that fine-grained information about electricity use, how much could a customer see? Seems reasonable now, doesn't it? After all, anything has to be better than once a month aggregate energy use!

So, the specter of smart grid data, interval meter data down to the 1-hour data and 15-minute intervals, being available seemed compelling. After all, with it, you can certainly show customers how their energy use varies by time-of-day and the day of the week. Yes, the data is probably at least a day old (meaning I can't see yesterday, but I can see the day before). No, I can't see the last hour or so … oh, yes … I guess that means I have to wait till tomorrow to know how I am doing right now.

So far, the results have been pathetic. Less than 2% of customers even attempt to understand the data presented and lose interest soon after trying to decide something based upon it. There are so few who come back to look at this data over and over again that it makes one wonder what we can do to get their attention. Contests might get repeat interest for a while, but so far even they have no long term engagement. Seems like we just can't break through that 1-2% engagement threshold. Maybe sex and violence? Nah, that is inappropriate.

When I am asked to speak about this to national electric utility management audiences, I summarize this with a basic question: "If the electric utility agendas (i.e., energy efficiency and demand response) were aired on a cable channel, would anyone watch it? Probably not!" We need to change that, and this book is all about changing that. So, don't lose hope. I believe we can, but it first requires us to stop thinking the electric meter is going to do it. Remember what I have said in the preface of this book. The electric meter is the scoreboard on the energy game, but it does not tell you how you are playing the energy game. But I digress.

Critics of electric utilities thought the energy engagement problem must then be that the traditional electric utility ideas were inadequate. The key to success would be to let the free market come up with value propositions that engage customer interest with these new smart grid meters. Google's philanthropic arm (Google.org) developed an online system (The Google Power Meter) to help customers track home electricity use in October, 2009. The first device partner was The Energy Detective (TED) with an energy monitor in the US. Anyone who tried to do this has their own funny stories to tell. This was a great idea on many levels...just not cost effective and certainly not reliably helpful in any sense of the word. Google abandoned this in Sept. 2011.

But, the fact that Google made such a splash with this and brandished their prowess across the bow of electric utility industry did not go unnoticed. As a direct result, the electric utilities made sure no one could read the electric utility meter other than them or an approved partner. The security around each meter became so tight that no one could get at the data, not even the customer.

The US government entered in to help. The thought was that customers (again, those 1-2%) needed to have easy access to this data in standardized formats so that their smart grid data can be made meaningful by others. This resulted in the Green Button, which does enable third-party digital agents to provide information to customers. That has not worked either. It is still a distant reality. Virtually all the energy companies around the world who have thought smart grid data might engage customers are disappointed. The vast majority of customers have not engaged, and if they did, they did so only briefly out of curiosity. Now they are gone and are even harder to engage on this topic. They have seen smart grid data and are not impressed. They don't think it is very smart at all.

This is not meant to imply that the US energy utilities have not made a huge impact promoting energy efficiency and keeping score with the electric meters. The results of these programs have been impressive, especially in California where energy-use per household has remained essentially flat in comparison to any other area in the US. But, the attempts to engage residential customers using meter-data to support their energy improvements have largely fallen on deaf ears. The vast majority of customers are simply not interested. They will fix up their homes and take the rebates and incentives, but they do not stay engaged when traditional meter data is used as the basis of energy opportunity presentations to them. They "don't get it" and frankly, "they don't want to get it."

Worse yet, when the electric utility industry does look at the meter record for all these investments in energy efficiency they are left with a nagging problem. Customers have "taken back" some or all of the energy efficiency improvement savings in comfort. They couldn't afford to be comfortable before they retrofitted their homes ... now they can! They suffered in the heat or cold in the past. Now they are comfortable and the bills are often lower even with this comfort improvement. The industry has known this was true and attempted to assess the level of this take back, but still waves their arms in the air every time. Regulatory proceedings over cost effectiveness of energy efficiency programs are still fraught with this peril. Neither side is happy with the inability to answer the key questions ... and they are very important questions:

1. How much have the structural improvements to the home done to lower energy use?

2. How is the home performing when the homeowner's behavior is considered?

The best smart grid data still fails to answer these important questions.

Therefore a **Meter Centered Paradigm** (**MCP**) is a perfectly fine point of view for billing customers for their energy use. However, it poses very real challenges when you try to communicate homeowner behavioral and energy efficiency improvement ideas.

Another related problem is that until there is a compelling business or customer engagement reason to move beyond hourly meter data, electric and gas utilities will not make that investment. It is hard enough to justify moving from once a month meter reads to hourly data.

There has been a huge number of press releases and grand plans and claims about the smart grid, especially in Europe where the decision was made to implement it country-wide in many cases. However, most US electric utilities do not have hourly meters for residential energy use today. Those that do have interval meters are really struggling with the user experience for the reasons noted.

Over the last two or three years, there has also been a renewed interest in home automation and control. The idea that a homeowner can know their home is safe while they are gone and adjust the thermostat and even open the door for a repair person, is attractive. AT&T, Comcast, Lowe's, and a host of others have introduced packages to do this ... but there have been very few takers. The Nest thermostat has probably created the most enthusiasm here, and that should not be much of a surprise given their design team was almost all ex-Apple employees. The price point keeps most customers away now.

There are occasional homeowners who install in-home devices (IHDs) that can indicate electricity consumption in 1-5 minute intervals; these are the same customers who adopt just about everything we talk about in the industry. They are the first to put LEDs in their home. They are the first to install solar panels. They are often intelligent and engaged, but as I have said several times already, they represent less than 2% of the general population! The point with the methods presented here is focusing for a change on the 98% who are currently disengaged.

It has been fascinating to see how difficult it is to get even the geeky 2% engaged customers to understand the complex electric meter signal. The big hope with all the smart grid investment over the past four years was that customers would learn how to better understand their home with this time-dependent, detailed, electricity consumption information. Surely they would become more interested in time-of-use and other creative time-based pricing programs. That has not happened.

The latest Holy Grail concept has been "if we could just disaggregate by end-use that hourly or quarter hour information, then customers would understand what is really going on in the home." Software can do this, but it simply does not engage customers.

Further proof of the failure of smart grid data to engage the average consumer is the fact that the smart grid providers can't get the customer to look at it more than once. Yes, they can push it to them in weekly summary emails and customers will open the email, but they still do not know what they are looking at. And even though experienced professionals might find 1 to 5 minute data interesting to look at, it becomes impossibly complex to understand at those times when the house uses most of the energy ... in the evening ... precisely the time of the day when really important energy-use decisions are going on in the home that a homeowner should know about.

A Closer Look at Electric Meter Data

The following data illustrates how end-use load disaggregation is done (to identify the HVAC system, refrigerators, etc.) and how these end uses can be identified (the signal for the end-use items desired) from the noise (everything else going on in the house) in the electric profile. Here is a typical one day summertime hour-by-hour energy profile of hourly interval meter data for the day. Hourly meter resolution is the most common meter data US utilities provide to customers. The meter shown here has resolution beyond the decimal point. Meter resolution doesn't matter as much at hourly intervals. It begins to matter at 15-minute intervals and can matter a lot at smaller intervals.

The vertical scale of the graph is kW in each hour (or kWh per hour). The horizontal scale is the hour of the day (one day of data is shown). The low energy use overnight is observable and we all know this is the combination of refrigerator(s) operation, lights and electronics being left on plus the phantom loads (energy used by appliances even though they are turned off). It is clear that this house "wakes up" at around 6 in the morning, but you can't know what is really going on. Clearly it could be cooking, lights, blow dryers, TVs, and who knows what else. Did the AC start or not?

You can't be sure. It seems like the AC is starting at some time and building during the evening, but you can't really pick it out.

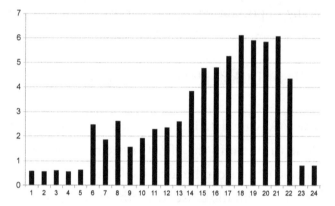

Over time, the day-by-day variations in this profile will trend with the weather so that the kWh in each day associated with the AC (or heating during the winter) can be estimated using simple linear regression, but it is impossible to know with any level of certainty how much AC is occurring on any given day, no less in any given hour. That certainty changes as the intervals are shortened from one hour, to 15 minutes and down to 5 minutes or 1 minute as we will now demonstrate.

Here is the same house on the same day with 5 minute data. Notice now that you can begin seeing the refrigerator cycling at night but can't be quite sure. I will show how there are times when 5-minute data can show this clearly and times when it does not. That depends heavily on two things: how quiet the house is electrically at night (i.e., is anyone awake and doing things) and how old the refrigerator is. Older units cycle more frequently ... while a new one might only cycle on/off about once an hour.

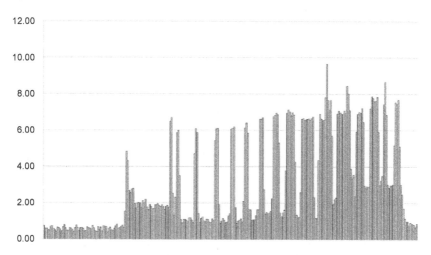

In any event, you can now see the AC cycling on and off during the day and running more and more in any one hour as the day wears on. You can also see the other loads (probably a combination of lights, TVs, computers, game consoles, and who knows what else) building in the morning and in the evening. Some of that might be cooking as well, but you can't be sure.

This home has a lot of noise starting around 6:00 a.m. and running through midnight. If we had a "quiet day" (i.e., a day when everyone in the home was away) at the same time of the year when the AC was running but nothing else was happening during the day, we could "difference" these two profiles and infer the non-HVAC and refrigeration loads rather nicely, but we still would not be able to detect the difference between the lights, TVs, etc.

Let's dig a bit deeper by taking a really close look at the meter for one day when the air conditioner only ran occasionally. It should be pretty easy to pick that out. And, by taking this closer look, perhaps we can answer the question: "What is the best interval" for smart grid data in general?

This question became very important to us when Control4 asked us to include our analysis methods into their in home energy monitoring product: The EC100. The idea was that it would read the meter locally using either a ZigBee protocol or the electric utility's preferred wireless radio technology. Meter data would be available to the EC100 in the home at almost any resolution in real time, so 1 minute data seemed entirely reasonable. We could use it and then throw it away after we computed what was using it. So, let's go with the idea that a local device could get 1 minute data. And, for the moment, let's not worry about meter resolution even though it tends to destroy the value proposition.

The first chart shown on the right is one day of 1 minute data. You can clearly see the refrigerator in this home cycling on and off in the wee hours of the morning. You can also see a spike when the father in this house got up to warm a baby bottle. Things like this freak customers out in some cases, and the folklore here runs wild with stories of folks fearing smart grid data because someone will know they got up in the middle of the night to use the bathroom. Folks like this need to get real … you can't see that on a conventional meter!

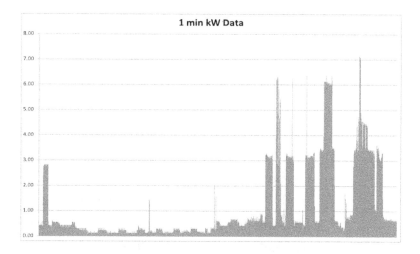

What else can we see in this 1 minute data set? First, it seems clear that the AC came on once shortly after midnight and ran several times that evening. You can also see that the AC ran longer that evening when it did come on … and it should, given it gets warmer late in the day. But, there are a lot of other things using electricity, and we can't be sure what. Is that the electric water heater coming on at the same time late in the evening? What are the shorter time duration spikes? Are they the dryer, the oven, or something else? These electric uses are almost all the same kW levels. These questions prompted Control4 and others to offer devices to monitor these indiviudal electricity users, but now the price of the installation is rising and the homeowner may have to hire an electrician to wire them into their home's electricity panel.

Isn't it also a bit perplexing to not know for sure what is the AC even with 1 minute data? Yes, and that reality should close the door on the concept of using the electric meter to engage customers.

Electric meter monitoring will never give you conclusive information here on an hour by hour basis and not even on a daily basis. It can keep score of the energy decisions in the home, especially over time, but it will never offer conclusive information that engages a typical homeowner on an hourly basis.

Before we leave this topic, it is important to consider meter accuracy because someone reading this book is certain to point out that 1 minute data might be extremely helpful in determining plug load and phantom load in a home. These are the electrical uses associated with things plugged into the wall, are turned off as far as the homeowner is concerned, but they are still using electricity … and in some cases, a lot of electricity.

Notice the gaps in the middle of the night when the refrigerator turns off. Why can't we track those low power use periods each day and use that as an indication of phantom load? After all, when a customer plugs in more and more electronics, we could tell them what they are using even when they think they are off.

Now we run into that meter resolution precision issue I mentioned earlier. Let's assume the meter registers kWh in each hour to two digits. The meter then records readings something like 1234567890.12 at a given time and another reading something like 1234567890.15 a minute later. The energy use over that 1 minute time interval is 0.03 kWh. That energy use in that interval occurred due to 1.8 kW of energy use at the home ... typically 3-5 times what happens at night in most homes. So, the problem is that what appears to be a very precise number becomes almost useless as an indication of phantom load even in that one minute interval.

I know at least a few of you are now saying you have meters with 0.001 precision. That means the smallest increment of load you can detect is 0.060 kW and that will kill your phantom load tracking efforts ... I know ... that is a real bummer, isn't it? Get over it. I had to years ago.

Yes, it is possible to calculate energy use from volts and amps precisely in smaller intervals, but now you have built a shadow meter to the one used for billing. The TED does that, and in fact, the data shown here came from a TED device. There are no utility meters out there that can support the 1 minute level with any meaningful precision. There is no reason for them to either.

Let's get back to the question at hand. Given 1 minute data is clearly not the right choice, could 5 minute data give us better resolution compared to 15 minute data? And, how much do we lose when we go to hourly data intervals?

The graphs that now follow were derived simply by averaging that 1 minute data in larger and larger intervals. First, the data is averaged to show 5 minute intervals, then into 15 minute intervals (the best smart grid data available in the US at this time) and then finally adds them up into hourly intervals (the most common smart grid interval data available).

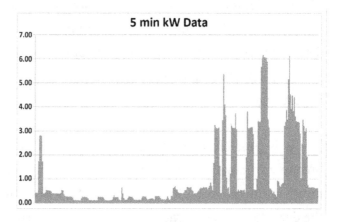

5 min kW Data

It is easy to see the refrigerator cycling on and off in the 1 minute data, and it is still clear in the 5 minute data. The 1 minute data also indicates some very short acting electric loads (often a microwave oven) but you can't be sure. Clearly, 5 minute data is a reasonable representation. It keeps the refrigerator cycles in view and does not hide the HVAC cycles where they seem to be evident. Fifteen minute data seems to largely wipe out the refrigerator from clear view and really blurs the HVAC signals.

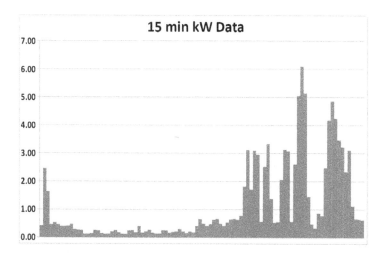

Remember that 15 minute data is the best available from utility meter systems in the US and is still far better than needed to implement time-of-day pricing schemes (since the price is never different in each 15 minute interval ... it is the same price for an entire hour). Does hourly data communicate very much? When you roll up the 15 minute data from above, you get the following hourly graph. Not very helpful, is it?

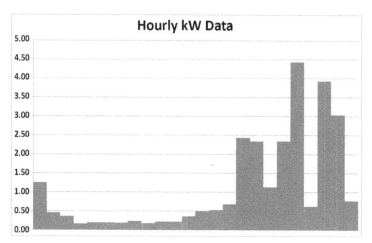

Hourly data masks almost all the details. Yes, you can keep track of how customers are using electricity and price those hot summer afternoons as high as you want, but it is impossible to reliably detect the HVAC operation with those meters, even at 15 minute interval resolution with any confidence. Yes, you can keep score, but customers will never learn how they are playing the HVAC game if you stay focused on the electric meter.

Our firm is known for detecting heating and cooling loads in bills and/or meter data, so I am sure some of you are wondering why I am so adamant that you can't resolve this any better.

We can accurately detect heating and cooling energy use in billing histories, if those histories are reliable. They are not always reliable, however. Rental homes in Florida … no way can we accurately detect heating or cooling if they are not rented for extended periods of time. Regression requires reliable patterns of use.

Said very simply, you can extract (disaggregate) heating and cooling loads pretty accurately when the home energy use behaviors are consistently repetitive. Natural gas bills are the easiest to do this with since there are so few extraneous energy uses. It is almost always heating and water heating plus a little bit for cooking if the customer has gas cooking appliances.

The conclusion should be obvious then. Give up on smart meter data to engage customers. It is fine to keep score and report the results of what a customer has chosen to do in their home, but do not think of it as a way to help customers understand how they are playing the energy game. It doesn't work.

Yes we need the scoreboard, but we need to know how we are playing the game. We need another paradigm for energy engagement, and we need it badly.

Chapter 2:

Thermostat Monitoring – The Heartbeat of the Home^{SM}

I t is interesting how long it took for me to finally unravel what was really happening in a home. I monitored our home with temperature probes for years trying to see this or that in the one-minute data, but couldn't. It wasn't able to be done until this latest generation of temperature monitoring technology was available with its high resolution and low latency. Very simply, today's temperature sensing technology has gotten cheaper and better. We are able to measure temperatures more accurately and more quickly, so small temperature changes are now readily measurable and very cheaply.

This is no real surprise given how computerized everything is. The devices are so small now you can barely handle them. They are also so inexpensive; you can hardly afford not to use them. The device we patented and built to monitor and control any existing thermostat can be built for less than $30 and it measures temperatures to less than 0.01 Degrees F.

The first time I monitored our house I was blown away by the clarity of the information signal that was now available. I could see the thermostat start and stop cycles without even monitoring the circuits themselves. That is, it was easy to detect the time and temperature at which the thermostat was operating by simply locating the monitoring device near the existing thermostat.

And, by comparing the signals from a device near the thermostat with one placed in areas where comfort was a question, I could clearly see what was going on and going wrong.

What was also compelling was that when you colored in the graph showing when the AC or heat was on, the pattern of bars was extremely engaging to all customers. It didn't matter if they were technical types or not. They know that thermostats control their HVAC system. They have never seen that information presented to them.

That is why we call thermostat monitoring signals the "Heartbeat of the Home^{SM}". As you will see, they pulse just like a heartbeat and show you how your home comes to life in response to weather. Once I started to take a closer look at this new form of data, it hit me that it was an entirely new paradigm of customer engagement. That is why I call it the Thermostat Centered Paradigm (**TCP**). TCP works perfectly well for HVAC and water heater energy use and overcomes all of the presentation and intuition problems associated with the **Meter Centered Paradigm (MCP)**.

Plus, given that the three largest energy users in a home are heating, cooling and water heating, this TCP is perfect since almost everyone has these thermostats in place. All we need to do is to help customers see how and when their thermostats operate. Then the engagement and education can begin.

First, the proposed method applies as a retrofit to all existing thermostats. The homeowner does not need to install a new thermostat. They simply stick this device to the wall near the existing thermostat. Second, this device and method focuses on the analysis of the two cycles in all thermostats that have historically been ignored: the on and off cycles of temperature and time. The best modern thermostats may keep track of the "system on time" but they do not provide useful performance information about what the HVAC system is doing when it is on. And, even more importantly, they provide no information about what the house is doing as soon as the HVAC system turns off.

The biggest "aha" you are going to have in this book is based upon that last statement. The most valuable information you can glean from a thermostat monitoring strategy is the characterization of the off cycles since they tell you how the home is behaving. We will spend the rest of this chapter explaining that. When you finally "get it" you are going to kick yourself and say "Of course! Why haven't I thought of that?" It still stuns me how obvious this is.

Thermostat Monitoring Terminology

Thermostatic devices are not proportional acting devices: they are either on or they are off. And, the devices they control are not proportional either. They run at full capacity until they are turned off.

While there are variable speed heat pumps and air conditioners in the market today, they are not the primary devices in the marketplace. Over 99% of the existing HVAC devices are simply on or off.

Therefore, the heating and cooling systems use essentially the same amount of energy whenever they are on. The total energy use is simply the time they operate times the amount of energy they use when they operate. (Energy = Power x time) Said another way, if a given heating system uses about 3 kWh of electricity for every hour it operates, energy use can be approximated well by just noting the hours the system operates in the home.

As a result, it is instructive and helpful to report total run-time in each day. But it is far more educational and operationally valuable to know the system run-time each hour of the day because we gain another intuitive attribute when we do this. If I told you that your air conditioner ran all the time during any given hour and it hasn't changed the temperature up or down, I can infer that it is running at full capacity. If the air conditioner ran 30 minutes out of the hour, it is running at half capacity. So, defining the operating minutes in an hour produces an intuitive and highly instructive attribute for customer engagement. No existing thermostat provides this reporting at this time. After all, think about what might happen on an extremely hot summer afternoon. The air conditioner might never turn off, and in actuality, the indoor air temperature might be rising above the setpoint. This is extremely helpful information. But, there is even more to be learned through analysis of the off cycles.

All thermostatic devices "turn the device on" at one temperature setpoint and run until they satisfy the setpoint that turns them off. We define "T" for temperatures and "t" for time, the most common convention used in engineering mathematics. Therefore, the data sequence is T(t) … which in plain English means that Temperature (the symbol T) is a function of time (the symbol t). Since the setpoints in the control system are fixed by the thermostat design itself, we will define the thermostat setting as the average temperature (the comfort setting the customer wants). The thermostat will have a low setpoint at T minus about 0.2 to 0.5 F and a high setpoint at T plus about 0.2 to 0.5 F. That is, the range in setpoint is about 0.4 to 1.0 F wide. Very old thermostats have been known to have 2-3 F thermostat setpoint range.

As an example, assume the homeowner set the thermostat to 70 F for heating. The thermostat would probably turn the heat on at 69.5-69.8 F range depending upon the age and design of the thermostat. It would run continuously until it satisfied a temperature between 70.2-70.5 F after which it would turn off. If the outside air temperature was constant and well within the heating capability of the system, and there were no changes in homeowner behavior, you can imagine a saw-tooth graph with repeating patterns something like the following. The heating system drives the temperature up from the on setpoint until it satisfies the demand at which time it turns off and the natural heat losses of the house drive the falling temperature part of the pattern. The saw-tooth will have a height that averages out to be the width of the setpoints and normally somewhat close to the comfort setting. The one shown here is for a 70 F setpoint and typical modern thermostat behavior.

Heating Cycle Thermostat Example Setpoints

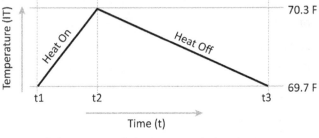

T(t1) = 69.7 F   T(t2) = 70.3 F   T(t3) = 69.7 F

The data elements that capture this thermostat saw-tooth shape cycle are summarized in this chart. The key to the analysis methods described later in this book is the timing marks t1, t2, and t3. While the diagram seems simple, the actual saw-tooth pattern for each HVAC system in a home is much like an EKG. It may appear simple, but it contains a wealth of "home health" information that can be extracted and reported to homeowners, trade allies, and the energy companies serving this home to help them.

The key parameters are the temperatures at which the HVAC turns on and off and the timing marks of the saw-tooth cycle. The precise temperature itself might be in some doubt, but that bias from the true known temperature remains essentially constant for any given situation. Therefore, if the device was reading and recording temperatures that were 1 F high or low, they continue to read and record temperatures that are high or low by the same amount over time. Therefore, the accuracy of the temperature does not matter that much. It is far more impor-tant to note the timing marks for how the thermostat is cycling and the differences in temperature between those timing marks.

The shape of this saw-tooth pattern changes as the weather gets more severe. The graphs shown here are for the heating cycle. Graphs for the cooling cycle are simply inverted patterns of these (the temperature drops when the cooling comes on.) Here the temperature rises as the heat comes on.

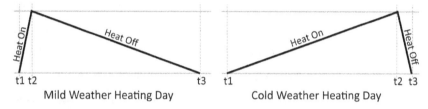

Mild Weather Heating Day   Cold Weather Heating Day

Notice how the saw-tooth graph shape changes for a mild day (when the temperature outside might be 50 F) compared to a very cold day when the outside air temperature is 20 F. The heater is running more often on the colder day, and you can also tell it is colder by the rate at which the temperature falls when the heater turns off. You can also see it is the slope of the "on cycle" because the heater is much less effective at raising the temperature. Please note both sections of this. We will be focusing a lot of time in this book on how important these rise and fall characteristics are and what we can learn by studying them over time. As you will see, characterizing the rise and fall saw-tooth patterns can identify and quantify changes to a house (improvements to the insulation, infiltration, and to the HVAC units themselves) as well as how energy use changes with home behavior (thermostat settings, activities in the home, leaving lights on, etc.).

Changing the MCP Into the TCP

It is instructive, albeit tedious, to convert the electric utility industry's typical **Meter Centered Paradigm** (**MCP**) for heat pump operation into the Thermostat Centered Paradigm (**TCP**) point of view. Trust me; this will really help you get over your MCP bias.

Let's consider a simple illustration. The customer has an electric heat pump unit that uses about 4,000 watts (4 kW or kWh/hr) whenever it is running ... pretty typical for a late model heat pump. If you don't like that number, pick your own – what number you use doesn't matter.

Imagine a very simple spreadsheet summary of when the heat is turned on by the thermostat. Each row in this table is one 15 minute interval time meter recording period. In this example, the unit comes on 10 minutes after midnight and runs for 5 minutes during that meter interval. Because it ran until 12:17 p.m. it runs for 2 minutes in the next interval. It starts running again at 12:32 and runs until 12:46, so it runs for 13 minutes in that interval and 1 minute in the next. The thermostat then goes to its nighttime setback of

65 F and stays off until 1:48 a.m. when it runs to 2:01 a.m. and comes back on once again at 2:40 and runs till 3:00 a.m. The table below summarizes the math and estimates the kW that would be measured in each of the 15 minute intervals which the best utilities in the world would use to bring this to the customer's attention.

Example: Apogee Bill Analysis estimates HVAC to be 4kW for this customer					
Time			Minutes		
12 Midnight	Tstat On t's	Tstat Off t's	On Time	kW Est	Tstat T
12:00 PM	12:10 PM		5.0	1.33	70
12:15 AM		12:17 PM	2.0	0.53	71
12:30 AM	12:32 PM		13.0	3.47	70
12:45 AM		12:46 PM	1.0	0.27	71
1:00 AM	Set Tstat to 65 overnight		0.00	0.00	
1:15 AM	So there is no gap in operation		0.00	0.00	
1:30 AM			0.00	0.00	
1:45 AM	1:48 AM		12:0	3.20	65
2:00 AM		2:01 AM	1.0	0.27	66
2:15 AM			0.0	0.00	
2:30 AM	2:40		5.0	1.33	65
2:45 AM			15.0	4.00	

The following illustration is pivotal to understanding why MCP is doomed to failure for customer engagement. If the best utilities in the world were to attempt to sub-meter this HVAC load and account exactly for its operation in each 15 minute interval, the kW estimation column in the prior snippet from a spreadsheet is the best they would be able to do. There is no better data set possible. Please let that sink in. Take a minute to do that. Otherwise, you are going to persist in the delusion that smart grid data can communicate the largest home energy uses.

The graph below is what the customer would see for each of the 15 minute periods early in that morning period. It makes absolutely no sense. It communicates absolutely nothing!

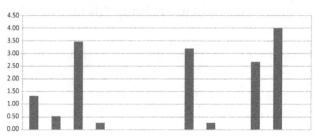

Even we energy geeks cannot tell what is really going on with confidence. However, if we were to record the timestamps when the HVAC unit did run along with the temperature of the space at those on and off timing marks, we do create a powerful and meaningful visualization as shown below (electric load is to the left and thermostat temperature on the right):

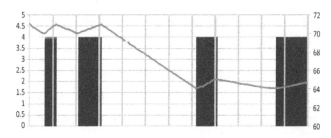

The vertical lines are the 15 minute interval boundaries that coincide with the earlier graph. They align with the time intervals for the bars in the graph above it.

I hope you "get it" now. If you are still angry and trying to defend the meter paradigm I want you to stop and look carefully once again. You have no defense. It is over. Meters do not capture what the home HVAC is doing ... it simply can't. It is the wrong paradigm.

Yes, it is the scoreboard, but it is a lousy way to think about the way you are playing the energy game.

Time stamping the thermostat and using this information to help people understand how their thermostat is really operating and when the house is really using energy this way is a "different point of view." And, the mathematical procedures, while simple, yield an enormous insight into the way the house is actually reacting to weather and thermostat settings that is transformational in our business.

Therefore, meter-centered paradigms simply will not be informative, even in a perfect world. TCP methods open up a family of analysis and thinking that can revolutionize the way customers understand a home's biggest energy users, the way energy retrofits to their homes are validated, and how customer participation in demand response is recognized.

Characterizing Homes In the TCP Method

The raw data is clearly a simple set of temperatures and timing marks, but we need to rethink what they tell us about how the home is behaving. For example, let's take a typical winter night where the temperature drops rapidly. The following graph shows how the saw-tooth will change over the night.

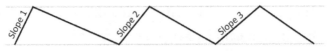

Weather Getting Much Colder

Notice that Slope 1 will get smaller and smaller because the heating system is working longer and longer to satisfy the thermostat setting as the outside air temperature drops. In addition, the time until the next heating cycle is shortening and the slope of the temperature drop when the heat goes off is steepening for the same reason. These slopes also depend upon the thermostat setting itself (which we, of course, know in this paradigm) since a home that is set at 72 F in the heating mode will cool off faster than one being held at 70 F. It will also be harder for the heater to heat the home at 72 F than at 70 F. Therefore, the house energy behaviors can be characterized by the time it takes for the heating system to achieve the on cycle and the time it takes for the home to bring about the next cycle.

Measuring these time transitions accurately can be achieved by directly sensing the closure of the contacts in the heating equipment or can be inferred by calculating the transition time from off to on mathematically from logged temperature vs. time at one-minute intervals. The elegant answer is clearly to measure the on and off time of the existing thermostat as it closes and opens the switch. Our system can and will do that if wires from those contacts are connected to the input sensing contacts in the device. However, we believe the widest adoption of this technology will occur if the customer does not have to wire this device into the existing thermostat to at least get started with the monitoring part of the customer engagement process. After all, most customers are intimidated by their thermostats and are even afraid to attempt to remove the cover to change the battery. We eliminate that barrier by the fact that just locating our monitoring device near the existing thermostat provides a very realistic and helpful level of information.

The following graph illustrates the sensing and inference method. The data shown here was collected at one-minute time intervals. You can see how the temperature notches up and down in a jagged line rather than as a smooth curve. The temperature sensor used in this graph has a precision of about 0.04 degrees F, and you can observe the granularity that results from that latest temperature sensor, in that our design has a resolution much better than 0.01 degree F.

Example of On/Off Cycle Inferencing
(Temperatures averaged over 1 minute)

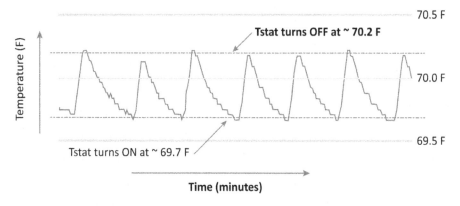

First note the horizontal lines drawn at 69.5 F, 70.0 F and 70.5 F. It is clear that the thermostat was set at around 70 F (and that is what would normally show to the home owner) but it is turning on at around 69.7 F and turning off at about 70.2 F.

Of course, the elegant answer is to connect the terminals, which enables the proposed device to act as a programmable thermostat by controlling on and off timing of the device. We believe customers will do that once they see the value in the added control features of the proposed system. It is also terribly important for this device and method to work acceptably in situations where the homeowner is tentative about doing so. This also assuages customer concerns over cyber security because there is no way the device can do anything to the home's HVAC system if it is not even connected to it.

An Example Daily Log of TCP Data

The following chart illustrates the raw minute by minute data for a typical day when the heating system is operating. The chart shows a 24-hour period starting at midnight where the thermostat was set at around 72 F overnight and was moved down to 71 around 6:00 a.m. The time when the heat came on is shown as a vertical bar indicating the heat was on and does not show at all when the heat was off. Around mid-day, the outside air temperature rose high enough that the heat never came back on all day.

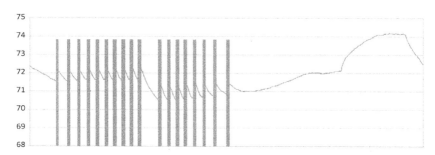

A careful reader will notice a bump in the temperature late in the evening. What was that? It was when we went into that room to watch TV and turned the lights on. You can even see precisely when we turned everything off and left that room. So, it should be obvious that this method can explicitly detect internal gain. Given how often internal gain is associated with comfort problems in a home, you can already imagine the power of this method to identify and confirm resolution to comfort problems.

First of all, notice how the bars for when the system is on in each one minute logged interval are thickening up in the early morning as it is getting colder and colder outside. Also notice that the space between the bars is getting shorter and shorter. Then, as the day warms, you can easily see the space between the bars widening out.

The graph below tabulates all the available data into an hourly summary of how many minutes the heating system was on, what the average internal air temperature (IAT) of the home was and what the outside air temperature (OAT) was at the same time.

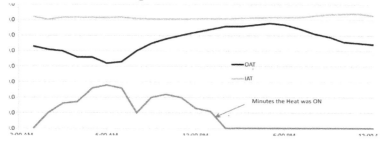

This graph tells folks in the energy industry a lot about the size of the heating system. Notice that it was running almost 30 minutes out of the hour at 6 a.m. when it was coldest outside. The air temperature at that time was about 42 F and the indoor air temperature was about 72 F. Therefore, the heating system can probably hold 72 F when the outside air temperature is about 30 F colder than that … around 10 F. That makes sense here in Atlanta. Oversizing the heating system is not as important as oversizing the air conditioning, which we will get to in a later chapter. Oversizing the air conditioner can result in short cycles of AC operation and humidity problems. Now we know for sure whether the home has this problem or not.

A tabular view of this data is shown on the following page and can be the basis for a wide range of analyses that historically puzzled and frustrated energy professionals. First of all, you can see that the coldest time of the night resulted in the heat coming on 28 minutes out of the hour. It was 42.1 F outside and 71.9 F inside. Therefore, the heating system would "max out" at about double this heating duty. If the air conditioner had turned on later in the day, that could be shown as well.

The heating system ran for a total of 219 minutes that day, but the informational value of that total run time is low until it is compared to other days and other weather conditions. It is far more instructive to see it when compared to the indoor and outdoor air temperatures.

Hour	Temp F	Main Living Area		
Ending	Outdoor	Indoor	Heat Min.	Cool Min.
1:00 AM	53.1	72.1	0	0
2:00 AM	51.1	70.6	10	0
3:00 AM	50.0	71.8	16	0
4:00 AM	46.0	71.9	17	0
5:00 AM	46.0	71.9	26	0
6:00 AM	42.1	71.9	28	0
7:00 AM	43.0	71.9	26	0
8:00 AM	50.0	71.0	10	0
9:00 AM	55.0	70.9	20	0
10:00 AM	57.9	70.9	22	0
11:00 AM	60.1	71.0	20	0
12:00 PM	62.1	71.0	13	0
1:00 PM	64.1	71.2	11	0
2:00 PM	66.0	71.0	0	0
3:00 PM	66.0	71.2	0	0
4:00 PM	66.9	71.5	0	0
5:00 PM	68.0	71.8	0	0
6:00 PM	66.9	71.5	0	0
7:00 PM	64.4	72.1	0	0
8:00 PM	61.0	73.0	0	0
9:00 PM	59.0	73.8	0	0
10:00 PM	55.9	74.1	0	0
11:00 PM	55.0	74.1	0	0
12:00 AM	54.1	73.1	0	0
Avg or Tot	56.8	71.9	0	0

It was fascinating to see customer reactions to a table like this showing system operation along with indoor and outdoor temperatures or the raw data graph with colored on cycle marks.

The one that engages customers is the raw data graph with colored on cycle marks.

This bothers engineers like me who believe the average person needs to see numbers or graphs showing how things are working in the home. I thought for sure the table or the summary graph would be more instructive. No, it is the raw heartbeat of the home trace that communicates best.

And, as you will see in later chapters, customers can understand that heartbeat rather well. They can almost "feel the house" responding to weather and to their behaviors in the home. They may not fully appreciate the numbers or their impacts, but they get the pattern. That means when they improve the home and they see the pattern change, they will know their home is performing better… right away.

Characterizing the TCP Over Time

While it is fascinating to look at daily thermostat performance graphs, most customers will be more interested in the consequences of their actions once they understand them. Therefore, since daily total heating or cooling minutes of system operation translated directly into costs, it is very helpful to report this to a customer. My wife's favorite expression for this characteristic is "dollarizing the degrees." That is, how many dollars does it cost to maintain a given temperature in the home?

Now we can be precise and with confidence. If you know that the home HVAC system runs for a given amount of time in a day, you can dollarize that operation. Then, when the homeowner decides to change the thermostat setting to reduce that cost, you can dollarize that change ... with confidence.

Notice, by the way, that we don't need confirmation from the smart grid meter to do this. So, many of our clients are likely to use the TCP instead of the MCP method to engage customers. This can be logged over time and categorized by the temperature setpoint in the thermostat. It only takes a few weeks of operating data to be able to cast the home energy behavior into an aggregate performance chart as shown here.

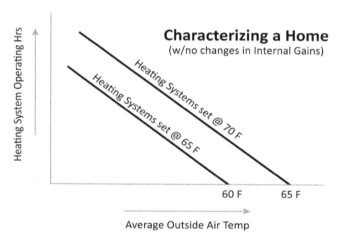

This graph emphasizes the assumption that whatever thermal gains exist in the home (appliance activity, people and pets in the home all day, lights, electronics, etc.) are all consistent during the data analysis period. The graph shows that for a temperature setpoint of 70 F in the home, the heating system data will go through the zero point of operating hours at about 65 F. That is the most common internal gain result for most American homes and is the reason **Heating Degree Days (HDD)** are computed in the US based upon a 65 F basis. If the homeowner were to hold the thermostat at 65 F, the data would go through a 60 F temperature point when extrapolated to zero run time for heating.

This is not theory. Actual home data does precisely this when and if the home-use behavior is consistent over time. And, this part of the analysis shown is not a new mathematical procedure at all. ASHRAE and other organizations have long recognized this operating characteristic, and this part of the method is well documented elsewhere.

Measuring Home Improvements with Confidence

It may come as a surprise to many readers that despite the enormous investment made to improve homes in the US, the results have been much less than theoretically predicted. Michael Blasnik of M Blasnik and Associates in Boston Massachusetts has published and spoken widely on this subject and is known for his work in this area after performing the due diligence on dozens of major energy utility home weatherization programs.

It is well known there is something the industry calls "take back," which has frustrated everyone. The home was so inefficient in the past that the occupants could not afford to be truly comfortable. So, perhaps they kept the house at 65 F during the cold winter months. Now that the home has been improved, they can afford to heat the home to 68-70 F or even warmer. Given that one degree F change in thermostat setting can easily increase the energy use by 6-8% on heating ... well, you can easily see how customers taking back some of the savings in comfort could be a big impact.

Historically this has been almost impossible to know with certainty. Yes, there are analysis methods to kind of detect this, but they are in themselves imprecise. Now we can know what the temperature was and what it is after the retrofits.

In addition, it is well known that some of the weatherization improvements have potentially disturbed the air imbalance in the home (since it may be easier to get at the supply ducts than the return ducts, or vice versa). The house may be tighter and test out well in a blower door test but may now operate at a negative or positive pressure when it did not in the past. The result is that the change in air balance counters the effectiveness of the insulation improvements. The method illustrated here can explicitly and conclusively identify whether the improvements are resulting in lower energy use and do so very inexpensively on a home by home basis.

Of course, it is impossible to back infer any results since the method was not in use when these studies were performed, but the costs for this solution are so low in comparison to the costs for weatherization that it is easily justified as an integral part of any weatherization project. The homes would be monitored for a few weeks or months before the weatherization was started and should then show almost immediate impacts after the weatherization was achieved. If the weatherization did not result in clear and appropriate reductions in the temperature change rate, the utility would call the contractor back to correct the deficiencies until the results were achieved. Again, any take back can be documented.

Demand Response Programs

One of the key reasons electric utilities have stressed the benefits of smart meters is to be able to offer customers time-dependent price signals to reflect the fact that electric utility costs (or opportunities to save money) are time dependent. The very hot summer afternoons often have high prices in the regional electricity markets. It would be appropriate to signal customers to that fact and share the benefits of reducing electrical loads during these periods. The same situation occurs on the coldest days in the winter for some electric utilities in the Deep South.

The proposed methods here offer a low-cost and verifiable way for these same electric utilities to promote time of use rates to customers who do not have a smart meter. This method documents the activities of the HVAC systems in the home. And, the energy use is proportional to these measurements. As a result, an electric utility could offer a peak time rebate for changes in the air conditioner setting and know for sure what the customer did in response.

This solves another major historical problem - free riders. Offering the incentive can now be conditional upon knowing the customer was using the air conditioner during the same time period up to the day when the incentive was offered. Customers who were already away from the home and who had normally set their thermostats to a high temperature while they were away would not be offered the incentive. The simplicity and elegance of this method is certain to gain industry adoption over time, especially as the regulatory and legislative confidence in the results are demonstrated.

And, as a case in point, one of the participants in the device test program has exactly that home thermostat setting. Take a look below at three days of indoor and outdoor air temperatures. You can see that this customer would be a free rider for a program encouraging them to set the thermostat to 82 F on the hottest summer days. Yes, they only set their thermostat to 80-81 F, but that is not the target audience.

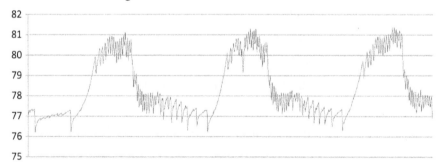

The best news here is that this customer would not be made the offer to participate in a program like this. They are already doing their part and justifying that decision by saving money all summer long.

By the way, take a look at how quickly this customer can recover the home from a 80-81 degree F setpoint. That is very unusual during the hottest time of the day. The unit is clearly oversized.

Comfort Problem Solving –
A Key to Customer Engagement

If you ever were to ask customers what they think about regarding energy, the most common response would center around affordable comfort. Customers want to be comfortable but they know that the compromise here is that it can be costly at certain times of the year. This is why budget billing is so popular. Customers don't mind paying a bit more all year long so they don't have to face the high bills in the winter and/or the summer.

But, comfort has not historically been easily measured. And discomfort has been mostly discussed with a narrative story telling approach rather than through a diagnostic and structured method. This can now all change given that thermostat monitoring devices can now be manufactured so inexpensively. One can easily imagine a fleet of these devices at all local libraries where citizens can check them out just like a book or a video to post in their home and study why their home is uncomfortable.

As an illustration of how discomfort can be easily monitored, consider one simple fact about the way most discomfort is handled by customers. They set the thermostat to say 71 F on a cold winter night and go to their favorite area to sit, read a book, cook a meal, or watch TV. The thermostat is probably not in their area. It is likely in a hallway or an adjacent room.

The graph below is for a bedroom thermostat with the simultaneous recordings from the adjacent bathroom on just one evening. The blue line is the bedroom thermostat which was moved up a bit when the occupants were retiring for the evening. The horizontal lines are 0.5 degrees F apart. You can see that the on/off for this thermostat is just about 0.6 F. The bedroom thermostat setting was kept constant, as you can see. The green line is another thermostatic monitor left in the bathroom adjacent to the bedroom. The rise in the green line shows something added to the thermal gain in that room. It turns out it was someone who went in to do some ironing. The combination of the iron operation and the lights added several degrees to the local reading. About two hours later another family member went in and ran a hot bath. You can actually see that "warmed the bedroom area" because you can see the heat losses go way down during that period of time. They then went to sleep and you can see the bathroom area gradually drift to lower and lower temperatures overnight ... there was no longer any heat-gain in that room. By early morning, you can see that it is a full degree F cooler in that room.

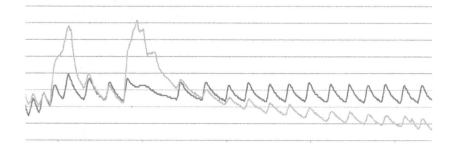

So, what do you think happens when they get up in the morning? They might be OK getting out of bed but then they react to the bathroom being cooler and … wait for it … goes back into the bedroom and kick up the thermostat. The bathroom would have heated itself up of course, but the typical homeowner is not spending the time in it to wait for that; especially when they had no idea what was happening in the home.

Don't get lost in the weeds. Stay with me and let this soak in. The TCM method lets us take a deeper look into the question about how internal gains impact the home operation. Since we can characterize the house during the night and during the day, we could see how afternoons with full sun might compare to afternoons when it was the same temperature but was overcast. That would prove how much that solar gain is costing us on cooling system operation.

Just imagine how this type of analysis could be used to compare the home on perfectly clear summer days with overcast days to determine the impact of attic heating on the home energy use. There has never been any conclusive and affordable way to show how radiant barriers perform in the winter vs. the summer months … this method would confirm true impacts that are otherwise clouded by the myriad of other factors influencing the HVAC system.

Imagine how we can finally know how crawl spaces operate and precisely why they do save energy when sealed. Consider how this might answer key questions about those problem rooms in the house like the finished room over the garage (FROGs as they are called). We believe this technique will become the primary way the HVAC and energy audit industry solves customer comfort problems.

Finally, consider a house that has been weatherized by a professional. Insulation has been pumped into the attic and ducts have been sealed. The house never could hold acceptable temperatures in the past and the customer is now comfortable. However, the energy use has not gone down. Why?

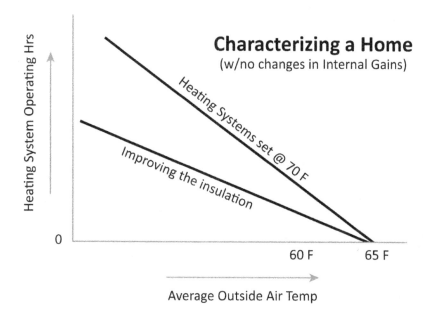

Simply measure the TCP characteristics before and after the retrofit. You will know what the temperature setting was before the improvements and have characterized the slopes for the rises and falls shown above. If the insulation and infiltration were truly effective (and you did not disturb the supply and return air balance that negated all of these improvements) you would expect to see much more rapid rises when the heat turns on and much lower slopes for the temperature fall when the heat was off. In summary, the heating system shouldn't run as often as it did. And, if the improvements did not change the slope of this graph, you now know it as a fact ... something that is still a mystery with millions of retrofitted homes today.

If the customer takes back the improvement with increased comfort settings that would also be easily verified and quantified.

Chapter 3:

The Changing Utility Customer Relationship

There was a time when the electric and gas utilities thought of homes and businesses was certainly recognized but the idea that customers had a choice in energy supply was missing. These businesses were monopolies and they acted that way.

Now, very few of these utilities would think this way. Customer satisfaction and the "customer experience" have moved center stage. There are even management level positions with this description in their titles. But, before we go patting ourselves on the back for all this apparent progress, it is important to recognize that there is still a lot of work to be done in the relationship to customers.

It is helpful to look at how the relationship has changed over the past thirty years. Thirty years ago customers would rarely ask their utility providers for advice about any home energy choices. Gas and electric choices were often made simply by the builders and contractors and those were often a direct result of incentives offered by the utilities. The sense of an informed energy choice was non-existent.

The marketing and sales relationships at that time were also pretty self-serving. An electric utility representative might be given a truck with refrigerators on the back and told to go out and sell them door-to-door ... and they did. Things were pretty simple back then.

It was about 30 years ago that the whole world went into energy shock with the oil embargoes of 1973 and again in 1978. The happy go lucky world was thrown into chaos and the regulatory agencies reacted with huge energy efficiency programs funded by "oil overcharge" taxes on all oil companies. The utilities were asked or even demanded to spin up energy advisory programs and to invest in energy efficiency retrofits. Some states, like California, took this to a very high level and have proven you can influence customer energy choices ... the energy use per capita in California has remained the same.

The style of the relationship morphed slowly from a product "take it or leave it" model to an advisory mode (where energy companies mostly marketed energy efficiency) and then to an implementation assistance mode (where third party contractors and equipment suppliers acted as agents to deliver the energy programs for the utility), which is where utilities are today in most parts of the country.

Along the way there have been several major energy bumps in the road. Deregulation has changed the natural gas industry into pipe companies (who transport and deliver the natural gas) and energy marketers to sell that gas to consumers. Some areas have seen electricity deregulation which followed a very similar model. In these areas customers were now mobile and the relationship might or might not include the energy efficiency message.

Peak demand management also moved along this migratory path which started thirty or more years ago. Electric utilities installed devices on home water heaters and air conditioners to manage extreme weather events by offering customers incentives to let the utility interrupt the energy supply for a period of time to manage through these peak events. Larger customers were offered special rates and discounts if they reduced loads for certain peak hours. Very large customers sometimes even gave electric utilities switches to their energy supply which they could throw and simply cut them off if they needed the power for system reliability.

But something has also changed along the way. Today's customers are less and less interested in energy efficiency. They have grown suspicious about ads they see on TV about windows that pay for themselves and all these gadgets that can somehow make their lives easier. They do not want another remote on their table; if the energy industry was a cable channel, it is hard to imagine many of them watching it. Plus, the weak economy has most homeowners resigned to living out their time in their existing home and perhaps even convalescing there as they finish out their time.

The basic pattern is set. Today's customers are harder to reach and the competition for their mind and their wallet has intensified.

Everyone wants their money and there is less and less of it that is discretionary. Therefore, energy utilities are going to have a tougher and tougher time keeping an influence channel open. Customers are getting weary of the constant bombardment by countless marketing messages. Watch your own reaction to the ads on TV. You are getting so fed up you would rather record the shows of interest and either skip past the ads or even set some recorders to eliminate them as you record them!

Customers are searching for safe havens and someone is going to offer them one for their energy challenges. They haven't quite figured that out yet, but now that this thermostat idea is out in plain sight, someone is going to jump on it to get this relationship.

Our company philosophy is to be the trusted partner to the utilities we serve and we serve a lot of them ... about 700 covering almost 40% of the United States. We will never "disintermediate" our clients and go straight to their customers. We always act as an agent within the utility marketing relationship to these customers, so don't worry about us. Do worry about others who have already thrown the gauntlet down and made it clear that they will go straight to the customer.

It is funny in a way that I am about to use a phrase that is all too similar and familiar to our long time client base. The book title may be a bit funny: It's the Thermostat Stupid … but what I am about to say isn't really funny at all about the thermostat. It is too cheap NOT to meter!

The reason that is funny comes from a period of time about 40-50 years ago when nuclear power promised to be so cheap that the electric utilities thought the power from it might be too cheap to meter. The idea was that the cost to actually keep track of the amount of power a residential customer used might not pass the business case to justify metering and billing it. That all changed about 30 years ago with one incident: Three Mile Island.

Now the relationship to the customer is under attack in other ways. Part of the change is driven by corporate decisions to change energy supply choices. WalMart has made a public statement that they will stop buying "brown" (aka dirty conventional electric power) in the US by 2020. You can call that bravado but I don't think so. Someone will get the energy supply business to meet their corporate objectives to do precisely this. Lowes department stores are saying they should take over the customer energy options business since they can make it easier for customers to act. They are offering home automation equipment. For a while Best Buy was thinking of using the Geek Squad to do that as well using the Control4 device set that our firm powered with energy analytics. Google made an effort to get between the utility and the electric meter itself, but failed in part because the electric utilities raised the security around the meter for a host of valid reasons, not the least of which is cyber security.

Natural gas retailers are offering solar electric energy to customers. Traditional electric utilities are thinking once again of district heating and cooling plants and getting into the solar business as a more active agent. Part of the driver here is subtle but important. They are not simply looking at the business as a profit center. They are looking at it as a relational center.

Will this happen quickly? Probably not! Will a bunch of folks fail at trying? Sure! My point is this . . . The train is leaving or has just left the station. If you are an electric or natural gas utility, please take note. Your time is limited. Either get this relationship under your control or lose it to others who do.

What Business Models Might Work?

I know what many of you are thinking. Come on Joel, don't try that ploy on me! I remember when the promise of deregulation was going to change the electric utility industry and all the best and brightest moved over to the unregulated side of the business because that was where the excitement was going to be. I remember when Enron was claiming they would rule the world with their energy trading concepts and that they would even trade bandwidth. Now those guys are all gone or in jail.

I am not suggesting the utilities get into new businesses at all. I am merely suggesting a very subtle change to the existing customer relationship. Remember, the thermostat is too cheap NOT to meter.

I like to harken back to the days when I entered the electric utility marketing business. I had been a field support engineer for a cogeneration development company and had, for years, reviewed industrial and large commercial inquiries into our systems. Day after day I would look at the engineering and economic performance of their situations and conclude that cogeneration was not their best choice. Heat recovery, a new boiler, or some other process improvement was always the better choice.

As a result of relationships I had built over the years, a firm who did electric utility consulting hired me on to build their cogeneration consulting business. After joining the firm, I changed that to an energy advisory business … after all, I had found that customers did not want someone pushing product at them. They wanted someone who would spend the time understanding their situation and needs and help them find the best solution.

I then offered the electric utilities a way to help their customers understand their energy options. Along the way, I built the first key account marketing programs around this relationship which became the backbone of those programs in the US. Edison Electric Institute hired me to build out their National Accounts Program which thrives today on the same agendas. The formula is pretty simple: build a trustworthy relationship in which all energy options can be discussed, evaluated and implemented.

In my opinion, the business model that makes sense for electric and natural gas utilities and marketers is to give customers these thermostat monitoring devices in any and all of the following situations:

1. **High Bill Inquiries:** Mail them a thermostat monitoring device for each of their zones. They simply sit it on top of the thermostats and within days our software gives the customers a full analysis of what is driving their bills up.

2. **Energy Audits:** Just imagine how much better prepared and effective an energy auditor would be to have data from a home before they visit. Energy audits can also be more persuasive and effective when the detail these monitoring systems can produce is used to explain the comfort and energy efficiency improvements to a home. Plus, once the homeowners make the changes they will see results well ahead of even receiving their next bill!

3. **Weatherization Projects:** Mail them a thermostat monitoring device for each zone of their home before you weatherize the home, verify it is worth the improve-ment and then verify the contractor(s) are truly improving the home and by how much.

4. **Regulatory and Legislative Personnel:** Give these devices to your regulators and their staff and ask them for their reactions and thoughts. Let them see how powerful this new information is. They will need to be "on board" anyway to get cost recovery if you move past the situations above anyway. They will quickly see and understand fully how this approach avoids free ridership and directly measures program effectiveness.

5. **Energy Efficiency Inquiries:** The definitive expert on customer satisfaction, J.D. Power, concluded residents who are energy efficient tend to be more satisfied customers. Customers who inquire about recommendations for energy efficiency should receive a monitoring device. The result will be a better understanding of energy consumption by the most significant system in their residence.

Once you have the pump primed with the above, it will become clear where the future opportunities lie. There are a host of others (energy system vendors, home remediation contractors, third party energy auditors, etc.) who will want to use these devices as part of their energy services. Perhaps your utility will partner with them using these devices to assure customers' satisfaction. Perhaps there is a value deserving a fee associated with that.

The big idea I don't want the electric and gas utilities to miss is that this is "yours to lose." If you don't want the relationship, you can bet your bottom dollar others will grab it. And, you can also go to bed knowing it won't be us who partners with them. We are the electric and gas utility partners only.

And, let's rethink the pricing options: The electric utility industry has been working on ways to link consumer behavior directly to a simple fact. The price they pay does not reflect the cost to produce that power, especially during the hottest summer afternoons.

Electric utility customers generally pay a flat price during any one day for the electricity they consume, regardless of how much or how little they use that day and regardless of the time of the day they use it. It has become painfully clear over the past two decades that this is not only false but when it is most out of line, (high prices for electricity in the market) customers seldom see any incentive to use less. The results have been devastating and resulted in a frenzy of attempts to engage customers.

The most elegant method is Real Time Pricing (RTP) which gives customers an estimate of what the future prices will be in each hour and thereby permits them to adjust their activities to reflect that. Large industrial firms have used this for years and some regions of the country have now allowed this type of pricing to be available to much broader groups of customers. Experience shows that few will accept this volatile and potentially risky pricing mechanism even though it can be proven to be a lower cost method to buy electricity. The budgeting uncertainties also can make it very difficult on modern businesses that get used to the lower prices and then find brief periods of very high prices with little ability for them to respond. This method clearly will not work in the residential market.

Some of the methods like Time of Use (TOU) attempt to do this with routine day by day pricing signals. For example, the price during all summer afternoons is generally higher, so rather than charge customers a flat price of $0.10 per kWh, let's just put the price at $0.20 per kWh for all electricity used from say 2:00 pm to 7:00 pm and all electricity purchases outside of that time might be $0.08. Theoretically, customers would benefit so much from the discount for 19 hours a day that their exposure to the high prices at $0.20 for only 5 hours a day would be a great incentive. The results have been abysmal and all too many studies have shown that customers simply self-select the better rate rather than change their behavior. In addition, the fact is that the price is not that high each and every afternoon during those time periods in the summer.

Critical Peak Pricing (CPP) evolved from all this by offering customers even larger price incentives for the relatively infrequent times when the market was at these peak prices … typically less than about 100 hours a year. Unfortunately, these programs are so infrequent that customers often view them as a form of Russian roulette so their concepts evolved further into Peak Time Rebates (PTR) where customers would be given a credit for anything they did to reduce demand during those periods.

You certainly can pick up on the drift here. Customers have always had difficulty responding to these programs because they didn't know for sure what they could do. And, when utilities tried to offer these ideas with communicating thermostats the fears of big brother getting into our homes limited that.

So, it is time to change the paradigms once again. Instead of worrying about what we see at the meter, let's focus on the behaviors in the home with that thermostat. Remember, we are not changing out the existing thermostat ... not even that old dial type mercury switch thermostat that can barely indicate an approximate temperature setting. We are going to let all customers know what their existing thermostat is doing right now and how utilities or energy retailers can offer behavior change programs to get customers to change those settings.

The essence of our suggested approach is that you offer customers time-based thermostat setting pricing. If you normally hold your thermostat at 75 degrees F and are willing to set it to 78 F during certain times of the day, you will get a certain rebate (based upon the analysis we can automatically provide based upon our analysis of the bills and the operation of their thermostat.) If you are willing to set it to 80 F, you will get even more, and if you go higher, even more. If you turn the AC off completely during that time and agree to not turn it back on until 7 p.m. that night you will get the most, which by my estimation could easily be worth $30 for that day under certain market conditions. That pays you to leave the house and go out to eat. That might get quite a bit of participation.

Note that the credits are only given after the results from the thermostat are uploaded to their online energy profile account … something that can be automated if the home has WIFI … and many do. And, given that we can detect if they are normally away from the home during the day, you could personalize the offer to make it "richer" for those who are truly behaving differently. You can now see how free ridership almost disappears. Yes, there can still be the occasional coincidence where the customer's intermittent behavior opportunity to have already decided to leave the house coincides with the high priced event. But, even here we can detect that no one is in the home because the thermal gain will show that. Spooky too, but we don't have to tell the customer we can detect that.

Chapter 4:

Demand Response – A New Resource Pool?

Anyone who has taken an economics course knows the law of supply and demand of free markets. When supply increases (at any given demand level) prices eventually fall and demand increases to intersect at the new point of equilibrium. When supply increases demand increases with a given supply, prices rise. These price increases can be dramatic in the electric utility industry during hot summer periods. Prices that normally hum along at $0.05 to $0.10 per kWh in the wholesale market spike quickly to numbers over $1.00 per kWh. Sellers may celebrate but the buyer is typically looking for lower cost options since they can't mark up and pass on these cost increases. This idea is the central tenet of demand response programs.

In many ways it is like the situation you may experience waiting to board a plane. You find out that the flight is over-booked and they are looking for a few passengers willing to take a later flight. The price offered is often more than the cost of the ticket you paid, plus you still can get to your destination. Yes, you have been inconvenienced, but it may be worth your while.

In the now distant past (i.e., before all the efforts to deregulate the electricity business in the 1995-1998 period), customers generally were offered one of three demand response options, mostly based upon concerns over electric system reliability. Back then the concepts of demand response were bifurcated into two very distinct groups of resources: those that could answer the questions of real time performance and those that fell into the category of "trust but verify."

They fell into three broad classes of demand response resource:

- **Curtailment:** where the customer contractually had to respond to an explicit request but the customer has already received the price benefit for a given demand reduction capability. Their price for electricity already had this performance requirement assumed into the price. The customer had to turn things off themselves within a certain period of time, typically minutes. Of course, the customer could also comply by starting their own emergency generator and shifting loads to that power source.

- **Interruptible:** where the customer let the energy company directly curtail their energy use. Once again, the customer received the price benefit for a given capability; but in this case, the utility literally has a switch in their control center that disconnected some or all of the customer's electric use. This was popular where customers had large emergency generators with automatic transfer switches.

- Time-sensitive pricing: where customers were sent advance price signals such as Time of Use (TOU), Real Time Prices (RTP) or other time-varying prices. These prices were set and known in advance for specific hours of the day, typically the day before the actual time.

The first two demand response resources typically required "two second scans" to verify the actual electric loads at a customer facility. That data requirement limited these opportunities to only the largest energy consumers (typically large industrial customers). These operating performance assurances were essentially a repeat of the requirements for the electric system operators to know precisely what was happening everywhere in the regional electrical system. Generating plants had no trouble complying with these requirements but most customers did not have that type of monitoring. Utilities with direct load control switches in residential and small commercial buildings could comply with these requirements because they already had scanning devices on the key substations to verify the load reductions were taking place.

In 1999-2001, many energy companies designed new and innovative demand response approaches in response to price spikes in several regions of the US. Because traditional long-term bilateral agreements were being replaced by energy trading, the newer demand response programs were modeled after wholesale trading mechanisms. Customers were now being offered price signals to reduce demand in return for a share of the benefits derived from that reduction in regional power markets, not just on traditional reliability concerns.

The result was that customer electricity demand response was now being traded against supply. The seller was now the customer and able to reduce demand. The buyer had become the counter-party who saw economic or reliability benefits in purchasing that resource. It was also resold into regional power markets, potentially for resale to others. Customer demand response was starting to look a lot more like the supply side. Economists were ecstatic!

But, all was not well. Despite these gains, there were major obstacles to the implementation of demand trading. For example, there were nagging doubts about just how real the demand response was and how accurate customers would be in their commitments to reduce loads. And, just like all other commodities as they were first traded, the acquisition and market clearing mechanisms were a bit clunky and inefficient.

In addition, the regulatory models stymied a clean break from traditional regulated supply to free market models. Customers were offered a safe place to hide at the same time retail energy markets adjusted to newly discovered price risks. Innovation was impeded by the regulatory attempt to protect customers, rather than permitting the free market to do that over time. The innovation all markets expect during a transition to deregulation was thwarted. This is still true in almost all deregulated markets today for residential customers.

There were also intrinsic delays in the transition to an open, competitive electricity market. One of these market issues was the lack of a common language among customers, traders, energy providers, utilities, and others in the electricity value chain. The translation of wholesale trading instruments into everyday terms and the formal translation of customer demand response abilities into standard trading formalisms was missing. Wholesale trading was complex and riddled with trade jargon. Customers did not understand call options and were terrified by terms like liquidated damages.

The industry was, and still is, a bit like the life insurance business in the early days. They described their product in terms that were technically correct by calling it what it was; death insurance. But customers did not want to buy death insurance, they wanted life insurance.

Along the way towards an efficient electricity market, demand response began to answer the key goals for any open competitive market:

- **Efficiency:** Economists describe this as the ability for buyers and sellers to find each other easily, come to terms, and transact. Today's end-use electricity customers generally have only one buyer for their demand response capabilities. Unfortunately, it is entirely possible that the customer's energy provider does not sense the same value for demand response as others in the market. In the future, true market-based demand trading among many market players (even customer to customer for large customers) can be implemented, leading to far greater efficiency. I expect several electric utilities to jump on the thermostat monitoring methods in pilots to decide which resources make sense and how to price and value them. They may then find that other regional energy players may value this resource.

- **Price (and Value) Discovery:** Today's single-buyer model for demand trading drastically limits price discovery. For example, it is entirely possible that the residential customer's energy provider only values demand response if it is available from 2-6 p.m. on hot summer afternoons. Other regional players may only need it from 2-4 p.m. Over the long term, the development of open protocols and standardized, tradeable agreements will enhance true price discovery. Thermostat monitoring has the potential to do precisely that given it is such an obvious and simple dataset. Plus, it by its very nature provides measurement and verification of performance.

- **Liquidity:** The ability to convert the transaction to cash is an essential element in all commodity markets. Economists call this fungibility or the tradability of a commodity because it can be readily converted into buying power or cash. As the reader will see later in this book, there are new forms of liquidity possible with residential customers that may prove to be much cheaper than the tradition of offering customers direct financial reward. For example, coupons to eat dinner at regional restaurants may cost a small fraction of their notional value.

- **Risk Premiums:** The identification and appropriate transfer of physical and financial risks for premiums is the fourth critical sign of an open, competitive market. Price protections are offered and traded in structured transactions in sufficient volume and according to reasoned actuarial data so that they can be guaranteed. Counterparties freely enter into and exit agreements (forwards and options) without fears associated with performance terms and financial accountabilities. The methods presented in this book will offer customer-specific price/volume risk quantification that has historically been unavailable. In a sense, customers will be offered unique agreements based upon the way their home behaves and how the home occupant is willing to partner with their energy provider. Buyers of these resources will have assured delivery of the resource by its very nature.

In most competitive markets, business risks are naturally shared by counterparties—those who see the opposite point of view about price movements. For example, consumers fear high prices and producers fear low prices. These views are central to the development of successful demand trading models. Market counterparties can strike agreements with customers regarding these price risks by shifting them using real-time pricing (RTP) or sharing them using calls, puts, and quotes. Call agreements are the closest analogy to the traditional curtailment strategy.

The key question now is how they are valued and implemented in the energy company portfolio.

If the energy company's portfolio is too small to trade directly into markets, they should consider aggregating that portfolio with other regional players or agents.

Managing the customer and trading interfaces for demand response is completely different from the supply side. With few exceptions, it is not the phone, email, and web trading platform business used by supply side trading. Demand response is more about building end-use customer relationships, educating them about their load shape flexibility, designing effective programs, and managing customer participation. These processes are neither cheap nor easy. Where customers are still under monopoly supply situations, it is certainly a challenge. Where customers have retail choice, it is an even bigger challenge. One of the key questions remaining to be answered is whether curtailment service providers (CSPs) can manage this in concert with their energy retail providers. If regional CSPs can make this simple, we may see an exciting new era begin.

Key factors identified early in 2000/2001 to the success of demand-trading programs involved adequate customer training. Here is a recap of what was important then and how that is now enabled with the thermostat monitoring methods. Points to consider were:

1. Educate customers about programs: Customers do not speak the trading language and are easily confused and disappointed as a result. Keep all structured programs intuitively simple, use plain English, and limit the number of choices. Now we can engage customers with something they do understand, or at least can learn to understand ... the thermostat.

2. Educate and test customer-specific capabilities: Customers who learn how to respond to these agreements perform well over time. Run readiness tests to help customers develop easy procedures to follow and understand their capabilities. Now we can show customers how their homes behave during peak days and they can learn what they can easily do about that. As they become more comfortable, they are more likely to release direct control of their thermostat to their energy partner. Fail at this step, and you fail completely.

3. Educate customers about markets and relationships in markets: Most customers do not understand regional energy markets and the trading and risk management challenges they present. This lack of understanding can lead

to customers assuming that the energy company is not telling them the whole story. By sharing the economic benefits of thermostat changes and translating that into easily achieved results, it is more likely that a sense of partnership will emerge over time.

Additional key issues for demand trading involve the measurement and verification of a customer's demand response. At the time this document was originally written for EPRI, gaming of demand response was widespread. Customers would bid on days they were already scheduled to be shut down for maintenance and even residential customers would sign up for HVAC control knowing full well they didn't care since they weren't home and the AC was already off. Now those free riders would be avoided with the thermostat monitoring methods.

In addition, the actual performance of the home or small business can be measured from the thermostat monitored data. A smart meter is not needed. You can know that the AC was set higher and by how much and watch how it operates. This drastically changes the paradigms for measurement and verification protocols in comparison to a decade ago:

1. It is intuitively appealing: Averaging the previous two weeks of non-event days to set a performance baseline has this appeal and may work for large industrial customers. However, its accuracy is not dependable for customers with significant weather-dependent loads. Residential customers are precisely those weather-dependent loads and the hottest days are also the days when they would otherwise use the most energy. Thermostat monitoring tells the trading desk precisely what the customer has done on that hottest day … even better than what the meter might indicate. In addition, thermostat monitoring has an intuitive appeal unlike the electric meter. Therefore, confidence in comparative performance can be known.

2. It is computationally inexpensive: Data requirements to document weather-correct loads were potentially costly and complex back then. Now that is easy and inexpensive. Individual customer weather corrections can be applied and settled precisely. A decade ago it was easy to spend more time on verification and discussion about weather corrections with residential and small commercial customers than the event is worth. No one would ever have dreamt that customer performance could be measured economically on an individual residential customer basis.

3. Each customer accepts it as fair: At the end of the day, the goal is to strike a bilateral agreement, not play a game of cat and mouse. Not all customers are the same. Not all measurement, verification, and settlement procedures need to be the same. Now it is possible to design demand response agreements specifically targeted to residential customer

capabilities. Customers who can pre-cool their homes to cruise through a multi-hour period can be on one agreement. Customers who can set their thermostats to 82 F can be targeted for another offer. And, cycling of the ACs can be decided based upon the comfort levels a home will sacrifice.

Customers and program sponsors often find that information feedback during a demand response event can be helpful. This feedback can be accomplished by interrogating meters and verifying customer performance during events. Historically, this was too expensive for smaller customers. Now, if the thermostat monitoring is connected to the web, it is entirely possible and certainly inexpensive.

If you are a forward thinking person (or organization) contemplating the future of demand trading, look beyond the current incomplete deregulation patterns that characterize current electricity markets. Commodity trading evolves along broad categories: resource development, agent relationships, exchange liquidity, and arbitrage trading. Customer demand trading resources expand through technology and information. These resources increase customer demand trading elasticity. But, they also require the acceptable standardization of trading instruments and parties who can trade them. Because smaller customers would prefer to outsource their opportunity, trading will also require permissible agent relationships.

Demand response trades will eventually be graded and valued along a continuum, much like stocks and bonds. Some will be AAA rated—better than some generators because they are already delivered, represent a large portfolio (so failure to perform is only matter of degree, not the zero or one it is with a large generating station) and will have environmental virtues as well.

Depth and liquidity of demand trading markets will only occur when the financial derivative instruments of risk management can be deployed as well. As the underlying actuarial data are understood, there will emerge a spectrum of price and risk differentiated products and services in the market. Demand trading aggregation will permit risk mitigation and rightfully deserved long term premiums. Those market players who move early into the thermostat monitoring methods will have a first mover advantage as they gain valuable market experience. And, for those of you truly looking for a real "big data" opportunity … this is it!

Finally, agents and the act of arbitrage will play a valuable role in demand trading as it does in all other commodity markets. At the moment, only the individual energy providers decide what the resource is worth. Customers will eventually look at multiple offers and decide which one best fits their abilities or desires for risk. Similarly, customers under real-time pricing programs with undesirable wholesale price exposures will find counterparties (surrogates) to take their place. This idea is becoming easier with Internet exchanges, but most of these exchanges are still many-to-one models with no standardization of demand trading resources. This situation will need to evolve to a many-to-few interchange in which all market players (even customer-to-customer) can freely trade with one another.

I expect these ideas will kick back in as the US economy finally begins to gain steam again. Right now, almost everyone in the market thinks they have enough supply resources. They are about to be shocked once the economy does pick up. The speed of the load increase will surprise everyone ... the buildings to accommodate the expansion of business are already in place, but are vacant or very low occupancy. The load increases during the next economic expansion have no historical precedent. They will surprise everyone. Those who can anticipate this shortfall in the appropriate timeline will make a killing on demand response.

Today's methods for trading electricity in open markets are still in transition. We shouldn't be too critical because these methods are still in their infancy. In today's markets, frustration can be so great that energy parties simply leave the table and do not play. However, those who play today will be better prepared to shape the path towards the future and will have learned a great deal about counterparties and their perspectives in the interim.

In this interim, an organization considering demand trading opportunities should consider whether their plans and actions are progressing towards open market models:

- Open market interfaces and structured transactions: Building the optimal customer-demand response portfolio requires transactions that are tradable to multiple parties. As such, they require counterparty acceptability and they must be fungible (convertible to cash or the equivalent in financial transactions). Just keep in mind that traditional financial incentives (cash credits to the bill) may be more costly and less desirable than discounts/coupons for meals at local restaurants or even coupons for energy efficiency items.

- Open trading protocols: Liquidity in demand trading transactions will require standardization, protocols, and performance assurances. These transactions should trade with price and value discovery, along with any other determinants that counterparties might deem valuable. As you consider demand response with thermostat monitoring strategies, pay special attention to the customer capabilities and potentially rethink/ personalize the origination process that creates the offers.

- Open information protocols: Markets only flourish when there is complete confidence in counterparty performance. Open information protocols with appropriate security constraints (so that private information stays private) can assure market participants of being paid in a timely manner for what they did and didn't do. Now you can be sure what residential and small commercial customers are actually doing ... or not. Plus, you can actually trade with customers who no one else can get to. Imagine trading with customers who have no internet access or smart meter on their home. They send in their SD card at the end of the season for a credit on their bill for what they did in response to your price signals! Trust but verify ... it works ... they were not paid in advance ... if they didn't do anything, you haven't lost anything.

Some might feel that the path toward an open, competitive market for demand response is too clouded with uncertainty, the restrictions too prohibitive, or that they do not have the resources to acquire and maintain customer participation. Others might view the trading of customer demand response as the "killer app" of energy deregulation (following the analogy of a "killer app" for computer adoption of the 1980s) and feel that these price-responsive, demand trading customers are the best ones to acquire or retain as energy markets move towards open, competitive models. We believe that the latter view is the best long-term strategy.

Chapter 5:

Residential and Small Commercial DR Liquidity

C urrently, most regions of the United States are experiencing took its toll and many residential and commercial buildings are vacant. Investments in demand-response resources can be difficult to justify using traditional economic analysis methods at these times. Benefits are often considered either too uncertain or too infrequent to justify building the necessary demand-response relationships and systems. As a result, many demand-side resources remain untapped. When power markets eventually go into constraint and prices rise, these resources will be unavailable for use. It takes quite a bit of time to engage and empower small customer resources.

Economists suggest long term price signals correct these issues, but there really are no significant reliable price signals for demand response in most parts of the US. Some regional electricity markets work diligently to do so (PJM, NY ISO, NE ISO), but these mechanisms have historically been hard to meet with residential demand response mechanisms.

At least up until a new paradigm in demand response was available as it is now with thermostat monitoring approaches.

Without solutions to the liquidity and other problems facing the demand side of the industry, it is likely that the U.S. will become increasingly vulnerable to the recurrence of power shortages and price spikes. What then, are the key factors needed to bring liquidity to demand trading and expand the demand-response resource in the residential and small commercial market?

Standardization is a basic requirement for liquidity in any market. Buyers and sellers must be aware of what they are getting or providing, and they must be aware of their obligations and rights. Accordingly, as electric customers are approached with offers to include their demand response into retail agreements and those capabilities are traded into regional markets, it will be necessary to use standard definitions to characterize the demand-response resources.

Standards must go beyond any one company's point of view and be acceptable to all counter-parties to promote commerce. Without this standardization, efforts at using demand trading will be inhibited by uncertainty and by unreasonable transaction costs.

This chapter discusses ways to formalize the evaluation of customer baselines and demand-response capabilities into commodity-like attributes that can be sold, resold, aggregated, and settled in open, competitive markets.

Once standardized demand-response resources are defined, different market players in a region will often value these resources differently. For example, some will value a resource only as temporary relief from high prices in the short-term market, whereas others will value it primarily as firm capacity. Additionally, a market player's perspective can change depending on whether it has a "long" or "short" forward position in the regional power market.

These differing valuations can help to drive demand-trading activity, but only if a customer's demand-response resource is accessible through open market mechanisms. In some areas, restrictions currently prohibit such a resource from being offered to any organization other than the load serving entity or the ISO/ RTO. Eventually, however, it is expected that virtually all regions will allow demand trading across these traditional boundaries. This will provide an opportunity for those placing the greatest value on a demand-response resource to have access to it.

In general, demand-side investments can be difficult to justify during periods of soft forward markets. One should consider, however, the inherent value of demand trading as a hedging mechanism to protect against periods of constrained power availability and high wholesale prices. While such periods may not occur frequently in any given region, their effects can still be disastrous. As history has shown, unhedged retail energy companies can be caught in an economic squeeze between high prices in the wholesale markets and low prices in retail contracts.

Unfortunately, many energy retailers are playing a game of Russian Roulette in this regard. It is only a matter of time before there is a bullet in the barrel.

Demand trading presents a way for an energy company to manage its exposure to this type of price risk. By having the ability to reduce demand during critical periods, huge savings can result. This can have a big impact on the bottom line – perhaps the difference between bankruptcy and simply having a bad quarter.

In evaluating demand trading's value as a hedge, one can consider the concept of "air worthiness." In the aircraft industry, this is defined as the ability to anticipate threatening situations and withstand unavoidable turbulence without destroying the airframe or harming those inside. By considering this concept in the context of the power industry, this chapter develops the metric of "survivability," which defines an energy company's ability to survive and gracefully exit the worst-case scenario in any one year. Another metric discussed is "staying power," which considers the cash requirement to remain solvent through a multi-year run of bad luck.

These metrics focus on the energy companies that supply retail power, but it is important to remember that the risk associated with price spikes and power shortages extend beyond the energy industry. As much of the country has experienced, it can affect the entire population and the economy within a region. Given this, the "insurance" provided by demand trading has broad social benefits.

In a perfect market, the implementation of this type of insurance could result in higher prices for customers that are inflexible in their energy use, compared to those that are flexible (given similar energy-use patterns.) Additionally, retailers that do not hedge their supply portfolios to meet their customer obligations could perhaps pay a premium when they lean on the ISO/RTO balancing markets to a high degree. In a very real sense, these retailers can jeopardize all market participants by their actions, in a similar way to driving a car without insurance.

Energy markets traditionally rely on forward markets for price signals, often using public indices such as NYMEX agreements as proxies for fair bilateral terms. Unfortunately, at this time, there are no such proxies available, and we are likely to see boom-bust cycles in the valuation of both supply-side and demand-side trades in a region. These cycles are highly disruptive because they inhibit market participants from sustaining a sufficient value proposition. Looking at the issue as if from the supply side of the equation, it is like no one wanting to build another power plant without assurance that the bills on that plant will be paid.

Given the current situation, a key question is what mechanisms can be used to develop the price signals needed to encourage demand trading. One way to move in this direction would be to eliminate the "safe haven" of non-time-varying Provider of Last Resort (POLR) rates currently in place throughout much of the U.S. These rates make it difficult for an energy company to successfully offer a risk differentiated rate. If POLR rates were required to be real-time rates for larger customers and perhaps time-of-use rates for medium-sized customers, it would help to level the playing field for demand-response and demand-trading approaches. However, this approach could be difficult to implement and might not be widely accepted in the current environment. Part of the problem here is regulatory unwillingness to let customers really see the consequence of their inability to be demand responsive. No pain … no gain.

Another mechanism that could be considered is the development of regional demand-response reserve banks. These banks would be places where customers could deposit their existing demand-response capabilities in exchange for periodic interest payments (the reservation fees) plus use-transaction fees as these resources are used. These same banks would also lend money for investments in additional demand-response resources, similar to the way homes and business investments are financed. Figure ES-1 visually portrays how such a system could work.

There are now companies following this business model in their own way. EnerNOC has commercialized this approach for commercial and industrial customers. Comverge and others have packaged up residential demand response portfolios following a similar model. Now, the real question is who is going to move to this new lower cost and increased flexibility paradigm? Stay tuned. We believe this will occur in the 2015 time period, once all the proof of concept pilot results are in from the 2014 summer period.

New approaches are needed to help demand-trading markets function with greater liquidity during the transition toward more competitive power markets. Some of the steps along this transition will be challenging, but all are achievable with a concerted effort on the part of many professionals and national organizations. Hopefully this chapter will spark further discussion and action toward the goal of making demand trading an important part of power markets.

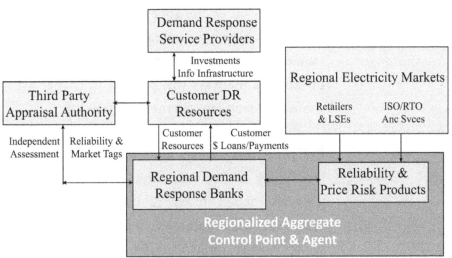

Figure ES-1

The Regional Demand-Response Reserve Bank Concept

This chapter focuses on the emerging price-volume-risk partnerships in electricity market relationships and how the measurement/verification/settlement (MVS) process technologies and information systems bring value to market counterparties using demand response transactions.

Market participants today have failed to pursue expanded value propositions because they are trapped in a cost-reduction thought process. This cost reduction paradigm cascades from a negative mood about risk taking and the infrequent/uncertain value for demand response. This mood has stymied the innovation hoped for in electricity market restructuring. In addition, the cash coverage pressures in the energy industry have also lowered the appetite for business risk taking with a natural consequence on expansion (and retraction) of business models. This chapter investigates the ways this is likely to change as confidence reemerges in the energy sector.

Everyone today is talking about big data. This area really is big data. The value of energy use information today is non-linear, multi-dimensional, discontinuous, and creates islands of opportunity (information based value) in a sea of relatively little value. The current limitations in the MVS technologies need to be evaluated against a theoretical set of price-volume-risk value creation opportunities, including the risks of successful commercial execution and the consequent market positioning. Don't just analyze the data … rethink the problem.

The opportunities identified through this process of rethinking will include the potential for disruptive technologies that are simpler and cheaper than the sustaining (mainstream) technology to enter the market, even though they offer less capability than what traditional market participants consider valuable. These technologies often provide lower profit margins and are therefore usually shunned by well-managed companies - which are often later destroyed by them. For example, almost all the MVS dialogue today is about more capable meters. Perhaps the real opportunity is for less capable meters coupled to an emergent internet business – agent software systems – to harvest the small or transient value opportunities otherwise deemed too difficult to acquire. The combination can become the disruptive technology in demand response. Do I have to complete the paragraph here: thermostat monitoring concepts fit this perfectly.

Think through a generalized transaction model for demand response trading that is broad enough that it can be applied to all electricity markets: forward, balancing, and reliability. To that end, demand response is defined as a resource that is potentially brought into play whenever the rights and economic benefits of doing so produce acceptable results for both the buyer (may involve multiple electricity value chain participants) and the seller (which is the end-use customer in these cases). The following high level outline illustrates the basic elements in the transaction sequence:

Perception (of an opportunity): When is it absolutely clear that there is an opportunity to use demand response?

Quantification (of that opportunity): At what point in time is the value of a perceived opportunity (or threat) clear both from a price and a volume perspective and the concomitant uncertainties surrounding both price and volume? Technologies and information management systems are central to this step in the transaction sequence.

Communication: How can the potential counterparties to a demand response transaction be made aware of the opportunity and then reach (and potentially negotiate) a mutually acceptable deal?

Transaction (the contract or commitment): To what extent can market counterparties transact on this opportunity? The seemingly elegant solution here is to standardize the transaction so that it is the mirror image of the generation transaction. Review of current practices and the constituent keys to success in these transactions highlights the two "sub steps" that have to occur:

- The ability to communicate and interact (negotiate) with any or all of the attributes in the transaction in a timely fashion.

- The ability to get a binding commitment in adequate time to be of value. As task timescales along the critical path are shortened (by technology and trading formalisms) other parallel tasks that were not previously on the critical path can now fall on the critical path. Unfortunately, shrinking the total completion time does not always result in continued benefit improvement.

There are discrete valuation and risk plateaus in the climb toward the optimum reward for demand trading. In a very real sense, picking the low hanging fruit does this. One might say you need the low hanging fruit in the market basket to pay for the higher/uncertain cost/benefits of the other resources you know you need. Appropriate MVS approaches can increase valuation and reduce risks, improving the net value of a demand trading business proposition, but do not cherry pick the low hanging fruit or you will surely get stuck in one of the plateau regions.

The real challenge today is not technology or even data availability. It is more about "visualization, monetization, and risk management." One can easily imagine a future world in which the trading desk is more like a fighter pilot's cockpit with heads-up displays showing key targets of opportunity and resources available. Once that era arrives, it is only a matter of time that the entire system is put on autopilot and is so easy to operate that any human who needs to intervene can fly it, and the industry can return to taking the electricity system for granted because we will have modernized the price-volume-risk optimization process into the very fibers of the delivery system.

The concept of commodity arbitrage in today's energy trading situations in the electricity industry needs to be expanded into concepts of agreement arbitrage. Commodity arbitrage is the act of trading commodities across temporal (time) and spatial (locational) value differences that exceed the costs of storage, physical transfer, or the time value of money. The current illiquid supply side situation results in forward prices that are primarily locked up in bilateral agreements. This limits the simple traditional commodity arbitrage thought process. When the industry finally considers agreement arbitrage, the concept that customer electrical use choices are the "mirror image" of supply side choices proves to be nonsense. The current paradigm in demand response that there is a single price market for electricity demand response is faulty. For example, how can it be correct to pay for demand response today and merely have the customer shift loads to tomorrow and potentially increase the price and volume risk challenge at that time?

In addition, the electricity industry has not yet adequately defined volume rights. One could say that volume rights are analogous to mineral rights in property sales. Most people never think about mineral rights when they buy or sell a piece of property. But, what happens when oil, natural gas, or even gold is found on that property? Clearly, today's paradigms about equivalent electricity market valuations are inadequate. When the value of mineral rights is low, no one cares about them in the trade. When they are or appear to be high, everyone wants access to them (and they don't want to pay much for that access). The trading rights for demand response are almost perfectly analogous.

The "rate structures" and pricing model traditions in the electricity business are still primitive and poorly defined trading instruments because the value of optionality wasn't explicitly identified and priced. This stands in stark contrast to the natural gas market at this time. The process of risk-adjusted value creation is shown for reliability business models (dominated by the ISO/RTO and customers who have to avoid interruptions,) replacement reserves, hour ahead, day ahead, and week ahead trading business models.

This evaluation approach points to "islands" of existing and future opportunity in a price-volume-risk space. It presents a method for visualizing these business models, trading across their boundaries, and the evolution of business value creation. The model also illustrates how stewardship and the supply/demand balance in the resource portfolio may be pivotal to mitigating regulatory risk.

The following figure shows how ISO business value depends on decision timescales and its connection to the availability of timely information, for timescales of interest to members of the electricity value chain. Changes in technology and operating practices can

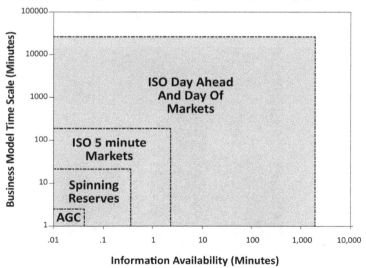

provide the means to enter or expand business operations in more of the plane defined by these two dimensions.

MVS is clearly a critical component of business value through its ability to provide appropriate, accurate, and timely information for good business decision making.

The figure below qualitatively illustrates a three-dimensional visualization of the islands of opportunity that can emerge due to better technologies or business practices that lower individual risk or operating costs, or increase business value. Actions on the part of one electricity value chain member can sometimes lower the costs for all members. The equivalent visualization in this figure would be a lowering of the sea level, which could well expose "sea mounts" of opportunity that could be exploited as new business opportunities, or business expansions.

Finally, the consequences of Location Based Marginal Pricing (**LBMP**) on the price-volume-risk interactions are shown to have unexpected consequences. The assumption was that these price signals would trigger efficient capital and operating strategies. Unfortunately, they have also raised the risk profile because the price signals are no longer as persistent and predictable.

Ironically, there now seems to be a preferred regulatory solution to reallocate costs and spread the costs across a broader range of kWh, and simply recover them through cost recovery. This approach impedes creative problem solving along the risk frontier by coddling safer (cost reduction vs. value creation) business propositions.

So, the conclusion is that there is real opportunity in this sea of current confusion. I surely hope I have encouraged you to seek one of these for your business. And, if it helps, here is what I believe is entirely reasonable right now even in the sea of confusion.

Apogee built the Demand Exchange Trading Platform to let commercial and industrial customers nominate the amount of electrical load reduction they would be prepared to shed in exchange for credits to their bill. Prices for this load shed were offered each hour by the electric utility and the customer would nominate the load reduction and calculate the expected benefit. These bilateral deals with each customer were negotiated either two days ahead of the event, one day ahead of the event, or in some cases the morning of the event day. Then, after the event, the actual electrical meter data was sent to Apogee and a settlement benefit statement was automatically prepared for each customer.

Customers participated in several ways. Some were offered prices on a best effort basis: try to see what you can do and the utility would pay in proportion to what they did. Some, especially the larger customers, were under true liquidated damages agreements where they had to produce the pledged response within a percentage and were charged for deviations from those performance marks.

Several of our clients using this concept went about originating these offers in different ways. Some wanted to fill a specific block commitment to offset a supply side agreement. Others simply wanted to know how much of their normal supply requirement could be "released" as an obligation so that the wholesale traders knew how much they could sell during the high priced periods.

Apogee's Demand Exchange traded over 300,000 MWh of this energy in the years 2000 and 2001 and achieved worldwide recognition for the innovative approach and the flexibility of the design. Since then this exchange has been largely idle because ISO trading replaced the bilateral trades of the day. It can now be reborn on the residential agenda by aggregating individual customer thermostat flexibility and time-based behavior changes.

Why should I think about this in comparison to reinventing TOU or CPP?

Why is this type of agreement different than traditional price forwarding concepts? After all, why not simply mirror real time pricing and let the customer indicate when they want their thermostat to turn up? Right? Why not give customers the option to select a price at which they will release their thermostat for a given number of hours a year? We are not arguing with those ideas. They are all classified as price-forwarding concepts because you are offering a benefit for a given thermostat setting or thermostat behavior. These are very good as far as they go. But, it is the subtlety of turning this around that gives you the added participation. Let customers offer you what they are willing to do in response to a price. Our experience indicates you get much more engagement and at a much lower price point.

What might this new style of agreement look like? Let's imagine it is the morning of the day ahead of a known heat wave. It has been pretty hot already and the weather forecast is really bad and is likely to stay that way for two or three days. Your wholesale trading floor has told you they expect wholesale prices to get into the $600-$800 per MWh range ($0.60-$0.80 per kWh) for sure and as a result, they are interested in buying back what would otherwise be a requirement to serve customers who are only paying $150 per MWh ($0.15 per kWh). So, there is $450-$650 per MWh clear value here ... let's round that to $500 to make the math easy here. That is $0.50 per kWh in the customer's perspective, and given we are typically talking about 4 kW of customer load available here, that is $2.00 per hour or about $8-$10 for the afternoon event.

If you offered a residential customer $0.50 per kWh translated into thermostat changes and told them what those thermostat changes were likely to be worth ... the day ahead of the event ... they are quite prone to plan to either be away from the house ... go shopping or out to dinner, or to think creatively. All you have to do is to offer the customer the opportunity.

Some of you are ready to pounce saying "sure, they will offer to do this when they were already away from the home or the HVAC was going to be off anyway" or some other excuse to avoid creativity here. But, let me stop you in your tracks. When you are monitoring the thermostat anyway, you would already know this customer was not using the AC so you wouldn't offer them this option. And, if, perchance, the customer was already going to do something truly unusual tomorrow and would have turned the HVAC off and you wouldn't have guessed it, you now have a firm commitment from them so you can comfortably release the obligation to serve the full load.

The basic idea here is the ability to offer customized, situationally achievable offers to those customers who are best able to respond and do respond. After all, you will learn how customers do respond to this as you exercise their capabilities.

It was fascinating to see how this worked back in 2000/2001. Our critics all said that customers would only respond if they were offered prices higher than $0.75 per kWh because that was the price they told them they would respond to. The average price for the 300,000 MWh of settled trades was under $0.20 per kWh! That is what customers did!

Chapter 6

"Things may come to those who wait ..."

Do you remember the rest of that famous saying? It is a quote attributed to President Lincoln. "Things may come to those who wait, but only the things left by those who hustle!"

The phrase I hear mumbled most often today when I talk to senior leadership in the energy industry today is, "Where's the beef?" Remember that Wendy's commercial years ago? The point was that fast food burger's had gotten so small that you could barely find the meat. Their underlying question is: "Where's the value?"

That makes perfectly good sense after almost two decades of the utility industry considering the business opportunities that deregulation of the electricity business was promised to unleash. Some chased the energy services business opportunity where the underlying thought was that commodity prices would have no sustainable margins. The gold had to be in the energy services side of the equation: Help customers manage the commodities they were buying by better purchasing strategies and through better operational use management. This makes perfect sense on the surface. But it proved to be much more difficult to sustain as a competitive business practice.

Some chased the power supply side of the business where the opportunity seemed to be the long term arbitrage of buying up all the generation being spun off by the incumbent vertically integrated energy companies. The thought was that these assets would earn better returns in a deregulated market where prices were to be set using the laws of supply and demand. That seemed to work well for a while and in truth may have been a decent business model in countries like New Zealand. At least, until you consider that the regulatory agencies thought that prices would be lower in deregulated markets than in regulated markets. That thought might be true when supply exceeded demand as was true in the 1994-1996 time periods. That proved to be a faulty premise in 1999-2001 when the opposite was true.

We could spend the next 100 pages recounting all the mistakes and missteps of this period of time, but that is not my point. My point is simply this. Today's senior leadership has heard of new business ideas before and they did not pan out. This same leadership now may be under financial pressure to improve earnings to cover increased costs and/or to provide decent returns to investors, but this leadership has not seen any silver bullet ideas that will correct or even make a substantial dent in the recent malaise.

Part of the current problem is that NOTHING will correct the malaise. NOTHING is big enough to correct the malaise. The base business is too large to be influenced by ideas like this. However, there are a host of things that are directionally correct and will begin the transformational process toward bigger solutions. And, more importantly, the business ideas expressed here are substantial businesses in themselves. They are sustainable profitable business areas.

Shouldn't that be enough to satisfy senior leadership: sustainable strategically valuable, directionally correct, transformative business models! I think this is more than enough for venture capital and private equity to jump at. And, if the incumbent players fail to move … they will.

Plus, these ideas reignite the creative side of senior leadership discussions. That is desperately needed now. I have consulted for over 100 of these large electric utilities and I have trained their leadership teams for almost three decades. I have never seen such a depressed group in all my years. They are beaten down and simply idling out their time incrementally tinkering with this or that. They dare not offer a truly disruptive idea or a breakaway concept. The current management preference for collaborative team problem solving automatically defeats anything truly creative.

But, don't get me wrong. Competitive retail electricity providers will see the beef with the concept presented here. They are looking for a product differentiator and this clearly is one. The price point is right and the relational value is high. These companies know how costly it is to get and to retain a customer.

But, what about the majority of the US electricity market where choice in energy provider is not real? These companies have to justify ideas like this with compelling cost savings and/or with compelling new business/financial value.

I am reminded of a workshop my wife Susan and I were doing for an electric utility on the concept of key accounts and relationship marketing. I had just told stories about how "understanding a customer's situation better than anyone else places you on the inside of the decision, rather than staring at it from the outside." During the break one of the attendees went to his boss who had brought us in and knew from firsthand experience the power of this concept and asked: "When is Joel going to get to the meat? I am tired of all this relational fluff!"

The manager picked him up by the scruff of his neck and said. "This IS the meat!" Perhaps that is the best way I can explain the thermostat monitoring concept. I understand you want the proof to the business case. I get that. Yet how can you prove a business case for a business that has not been built yet? My personal favorite innovator is Steve Jobs who also said: "For something this complicated, it's really hard to design products by focus groups. A lot of times, people don't know what they want until you show it to them."

I am showing you and you need to show your customers. Steve Jobs created more new classes of electronic devices that customers didn't even know they needed. Think about the time before the iPod when we thought you had to use tapes or CDs for music. The iTunes online store is now a very big business. He was working on the iPad ahead of the iPhone ... two more transformational device categories.

I am not implying I am a Steve Jobs. But what I am pleading with those of you in the energy utility side of this business to consider is that quote from Abraham Lincoln because, if you wait too long, many others who want to replace or supplant your relationship will move in on this opportunity. That is why I came to many of you first with the announcement of this concept way before this book was even being written. That is why I introduced this book to the industry partners who cover and follow all the competitive movements in the energy industry. I want the natural partner to residential and small commercial customers to consider this opportunity first.

I hate fear mongering as the basis for doing anything, but I have to admit that pain and fear are the best ways to move this industry into action. I transformed the energy industry about 30 years ago with my book on cogeneration wherein I emphasized that the energy industry should neither be for nor against the concept. If it is in the best interest of the customer, the energy industry should help customers make this decision carefully. Cogeneration vendors at the time had their own interests at the top of their agendas. Cogeneration was, and still is, not the best energy supply answer for most customers. That effort on my part transformed the cogeneration industry completely and caused hundreds of electricity utilities to spin up key account relationships. Yes, I wrote the defining books on both topics.

I am watching another battle brewing at the customer interface. We watched Google enter at the meter level. Yes they failed, but they certainly weren't fooling around. Now we are watching AT&T, home security companies, Lowe's, Nest, and others circling around the thermostat opportunity. They are thinking retrofit and that makes sense given the business structures they have. They are moving towards home energy management and getting between the utility and their customers. I am suggesting a completely different approach in that it uses the existing thermostat and thereby that cuts across the vast majority of customers. Plus, my suggested approach brings about consumer education and engagement and that is what is truly needed.

So, you might use that as the justification for action. Go ahead, but I have some bigger ideas that I believe are central to the future of the industry. There are just three of them and they are very easy to internalize, so let me close this book with them.

Rebuild the Regulatory/Legislative Relationships: Utilities have been increasingly at odds with their regulatory and legislative counterparties in regional energy markets. There has been a growing distrust over the value of smart grid, the effectiveness of energy efficiency programs, the value of demand response and creative pricing programs, etc. It is time to stop the bickering and look at the real facts. It is time to use the thermostat monitoring approach to truly answer or at least open up the better questions for dialogue. We can now know whether a customer is a potential free rider before we even offer them a program opportunity. We can also know the extent to which a home has been improved and the degree to which customers have taken back the savings in comfort.

Expand the Smart Grid Paradigms: It is high time that the industry stops thinking the presenting electric meter data is going to engage the average customer. As this book has repeatedly emphasized, watching the scoreboard is not going to change the way the game is played. Plus, for those of you who have yet to bite the smart grid bullet, thermostat monitoring holds much of the promise of customer influence at a small fraction of the cost.

New Information Highway and Real Value for Big Data: Do you remember when the early advocates of the internet pointed to it as the information superhighway … the infobahn? No one questions the value any longer. If anything, it may be too good as a superhighway given how bad information can sweep through the world. The latest buzz has been around smart grid data as a wealth of information. It is big data in terms of size, but it is so filled with noise that real signal value is hard to find. This book has offered just a few gold nuggets of value. They are diamonds in the rough. Many more will be uncovered. Some will be stunning and we will once again wonder: "Why couldn't I see that?"

To me, I am thrilled to open up these and other related discussions and dialogues to this fresh approach. When I entered the electricity marketing game about thirty years ago it was brimming with new ideas and excitement around energy efficiency, demand response, and creative pricing. Industry meetings were fascinating collegiate gatherings of brilliant creative thinkers who jousted about trying new things.

Industry meetings have grown stale. We now simply revisit old ideas with new labels such as "the customer experience." We still talk about mobile as if it were a distant planet we might want to visit. We try to keep prepaid energy in the small box defined by customers who are credit challenged. We fail to see business value in nascent informational platforms.

Please join me in moving this back into an exciting industry to be a part of. I believe it is. You probably do as well, or you would have stopped reading a long time ago.